D0932734

Whole Child, Whole School

Applying Theory to Practice in a Community School

TOURO COLLEGE LIBRARY
Kings Hwy

Eileen Santiago, JoAnne Ferrara, and Jane Quinn

WITHDRAWN

ROWMAN & LITTLEFIELD EDUCATION

A division of
ROWMAN & LITTLEFIELD PUBLISHERS, INC.
Lanham • New York • Toronto • Plymouth, UK

KH

Published by Rowman & Littlefield Education
A division of Rowman & Littlefield Publishers, Inc.
A wholly owned subsidiary of The Rowman & Littlefield Publishing Group, Inc.
4501 Forbes Boulevard, Suite 200, Lanham, Maryland 20706
www.rowman.com

10 Thornbury Road, Plymouth PL6 7PP, United Kingdom

Copyright © 2012 by Eileen Santiago, JoAnne Ferrara, and Jane Quinn

All rights reserved. No part of this book may be reproduced in any form or by any electronic or mechanical means, including information storage and retrieval systems, without written permission from the publisher, except by a reviewer who may quote passages in a review.

British Library Cataloguing in Publication Information Available

Library of Congress Cataloging-in-Publication Data Available

ISBN 978-1-61048-606-4 (cloth : alk. paper) ISBN 978-1-61048-607-1 (paper : alk. paper)

∞™ The paper used in this publication meets the minimum requirements of American National Standard for Information Sciences—Permanence of Paper for Printed Library Materials, ANSI/NISO Z39.48-1992.

Printed in the United States of America

8/28/13

"Community schools are schools that never sleep, caring about and working to support all children and all families."

Fifth-grade teacher from the Thomas Edison Elementary School

This book is dedicated to our husbands—George Santiago, Frank Ferrara (and the kids), and Terry Quinn—in appreciation of their endless support; to the memory of Joy Dryfoos, for having guided the work of community school practitioners for more than a generation; and to the Thomas Edison School community and its partners for improving the lives of children and families.

Contents

Foreword: Responding Holistically to the Needs of Immigrant Children

Dr. Pedro A. Noguera, New York University

Children of recent immigrants constitute the fastest growing population among school-age children in the United States (NCES, 2007), and all indicators suggest that their numbers will continue to grow. Regardless of how many guards are deployed at the border or how many fences are built, it appears highly unlikely that immigrants, both legal and undocumented, will be deterred from finding ways to enter and settle in the United States. The imbalance in wealth between the nations of North and South America, the persistent demand of the U.S. economy for cheap labor, and the desperate conditions in many of the villages and towns in Mexico and Central America make it inevitable that immigrants will do whatever it takes to continue to come to the United States. They will come for the same reasons that Irish, Italian, German, Polish, and other immigrants came to the United States before—because they perceive this country as a land of opportunity and a place where they can better their lives.

Just as we can be sure that immigrants will continue to come to the United States in large numbers, we can also be sure that their children will end up in our nation's public schools. As has been true for every other generation of immigrants, it will be left to the public schools to figure out how to absorb, acculturate, and educate immigrant children (Fass, 2007). Changes in the demographic makeup of the nation's public schools are occurring at a dramatic pace. In states such as California, Texas, and Florida, new immigrants make up over a third of the student population (Ruiz-de-Valasco et al., 2001). In major cities such as New York, Miami, and Los Angeles, they comprise over 40 percent of the student population (Kohler and Lazarin, 2007). Similar changes are occurring in small towns and rural areas throughout the United States. Thus far, the courts have ruled that *all* children, even those who are undocumented, have a right to an education (*Plyler v. Doe*, 457 U.S. 202,

221, 1982). For this reason, those interested in understanding how the nation will be changed as a result of immigration would be wise to look first to our public schools to understand how these changes are playing out.

As immigrant children enroll in our nation's public schools, educators are compelled to figure out how to meet their educational and social needs. Though the primary need may seem to be the need to learn the English language, schools serving large populations of immigrant children are faced with a double challenge: their students must also learn content across the academic disciplines, and they must learn to navigate a new culture. Research on immigrant children has shown that meeting this challenge can be extremely difficult. In addition to developing communicative English language proficiency, there is a need to simultaneously build content literacies for English language learners (Wells, 1994), many of whom also have low cognitive academic language proficiency skills (CALP) (August et al., 2006; Chamot, 1994; García et al., 1995). In many cases, students may gain sufficient proficiency in the English language to exit an English as a Second Language (ESL) program after three years, but for most students it can take between five to seven years to become fully competent in both communicative and academic discourse (Cummins, 1981).

Furthermore, young children of immigrants face multiple disadvantages that place them at risk for school failure, and the risks facing immigrant children extend well beyond their legal status. Recent research on the status of immigrants has shown that while the children of immigrants are more likely to live in two-parent families than children born to nonimmigrant parents (Capps et al., 2004), they are also more likely to live in households with incomes that fall below the poverty level and that lack health insurance and stable housing (Capps et al., 2004; Fix, 2001; Guendelman et al., 2001) than children whose parents were both born in the United States. Immigrant children are also more likely to attend segregated schools and schools that are poorly funded (Orfield and Eaton, 1996). Fifty-six percent of immigrant children come from low-income families and compared to 19 percent of children born to U.S.-born parents (Capps et al., 2004). Children of immigrants are also 50 percent less likely to receive temporary assistance for needy families (TANF) and about twice as likely to be in poor health (Capps et al., 2004; Takanishi, 2004).

Despite these harsh realities, there are a small number of elementary schools that have implemented reforms that address some of the challenges involved with educating immigrant children, and they have achieved remarkable results. This study documents strategies that were used by one such school and the changes that were produced over the course of several years. What the reader will find to be most important about this case is not the particular reforms that were chosen but how their thoughtful and deliberate implementation and alignment to each other produced a transformative effect upon the school and student learning. The fact that this school served immigrant children from families in poverty makes the story of how they achieved success that much more remarkable.

At a time when educators and policymakers are searching for ways to turn around unsuccessful schools, it would be wise to learn from the experiences of schools like this one that has managed to be so successful in raising the literacy levels of its students. Particularly given that most schools across the United States that serve similar populations are struggling, the lessons to be gained here are all the more important. It is still too common to encounter articles and news stories lamenting the low academic achievement of immigrant students, particularly Latinos. This is the story of a neighborhood school that takes in all children who live in the surrounding neighborhood regardless of their need, status, or circumstance. It serves them well because it takes the time to fully understand who they are and what they need. It is a profound lesson that educators and policymakers throughout the United States should learn from.

REFERENCES

Capps, R., Fix, M., Ost, J., Reardon-Anderson, J., and Passel, J. S. (2004). *The health and well-being of young children of immigrants*. Washington, DC: Urban Institute.

Fass, P. S. (2007). *Children of a new world: Society, culture, and globalization*. New York: New York University Press.

Guendelman, S., Schauffler, H. H., and Pearl, M. (2001). Unfriendly shores: How immigrant children fare in the U.S. health system. *Health Affairs 20*(1): 257–66.

Kohler, A., and Lazarin, M. (2007). *Hispanic education in the United States: Statistical brief.* Washington, DC: National Council of La Raza.

Orfield, G., and Eaton, S. (1996). *Dismantling desegregation: The quiet reversal of Brown v. Board of Education*. New York: New Press.

Ruiz-de-Valasco, J., Fix, M., and Clewell, B. C. (2001). *Overlooked and underserved: Immigrant students in U.S. secondary schools*. Washington, DC: Urban Institute.

Takanishi, R. (2004). Leveling the playing field: Supporting immigrant children from birth to eight. *The Future of Children, 14*(2).

Acknowledgments

The authors acknowledge the many individuals who helped create a vision for community schools. Their eagerness to share time, expertise, and resources transformed the Thomas Edison Elementary School into a vibrant hub of services and programs for children and families. First and foremost, we thank Congresswoman Nita Lowey for her ongoing support of the community school model at Edison and Congressman Steny Hoyer for the strong role he has played in advocating for community schools at the national level.

We also wish to thank Dr. Charles Colletti, former Port Chester Schools superintendent, for his leadership and willingness to implement the district's first community school at Edison, and Cora Greenberg of the Westchester Children's Association and the late Joy Dryfoos for helping launch this initiative.

We deeply appreciate the important role played by the national Coalition for Community Schools for disseminating their vast knowledge and experience in the field, offering their encouragement, and including our work in their national conferences. A special thank you also goes to the New York University Metropolitan Center for Urban Education (NYU Metro Center) for their research and dissemination efforts on the importance of addressing the needs of children growing up in poverty. We also thank the Children's Aid Society's National Center for Community Schools, not only for agreeing to partner on this book but also for providing technical assistance throughout our implementation work at Edison and for including our school in study visits for educators from across the country and, indeed, the world.

We are grateful to those early partners including SER of Westchester, The Guidance Center, the Open Door Family Medical Centers, the Board of Co-operative Educational Services of Southern Westchester (BOCES), and Manhattanville College for their commitment to the children and families at the

Edison School and for bringing vital services and programs to the school site where they could be easily accessed. We thank Shelley Wepner, dean of the School of Education at Manhattanville College, for her unending support of the professional development school at Edison, as well as the countless pre-service teachers from the college who worked alongside Edison teachers to provide quality instruction to the children.

Finally, we thank the staff at Edison for working tirelessly with Dr. Eileen Santiago from 1996 to 2011, during her tenure as the principal of the Thomas Edison Elementary School, to bring the community school vision into a reality, and to the parents for believing in the power of the community school to address their needs and the needs of their children.

Chapter One

Addressing the Needs of Children Lost in Our Public Schools by Embracing the Whole Child

INTRODUCTION

Policymakers, educators, and the general public expected the twenty-first century to usher in school reform initiatives that would ameliorate the social inequities for children growing up in poverty and improve opportunities for their academic success and socioeconomic advancement. However, similar to the disappointment of a New Year's resolution that has not been fulfilled, we are still confronted by the same challenges, and many of our public schools continue the struggle to eliminate the achievement gap that still exists between poor students and their middle-class counterparts, perpetuating a system of schooling that has lost many of our children in the process.

With an expansion of the term *urban* to include the many schools with a relatively poor and nonwhite student population, regardless of their geographic location (Noguera, 2003), how schools are organized and the services they provide have thus failed to keep pace with the diversity of the children they serve. From school choice options to merit pay for teachers, school districts around the country still struggle to explore new avenues of school reform aimed at improving student outcomes.

Community schools have emerged over the last two decades as a promising reform effort for responding to the effects of immigration and poverty in ways that have not been addressed by other reform models. This book about community schools represents a coming together of the theoretical, practical, and policy perspectives offered by the authors: the former principal of the Thomas Edison Elementary School in Port Chester, New York; a teacher educator from Manhattanville College, a local institution that partnered with this school; and the director of the National Center for Community Schools, a national expert who has studied the relationship between public policies and educational practices in community schools across the country.

Our purpose is to give the reader a greater understanding of "Whole Child Education" and its place in designing school programs and services in a more comprehensive and integrated way than have traditionally occurred in most schools. This book also introduces the community school as a strategy for providing Whole Child Education, closely examining the journey of the Thomas Edison Elementary School (often simply referred to in this book as "Edison") in moving forward with adopting and adapting this unique approach to school reform and improvement.

As authors, we describe how the common concerns of school practitioners at Edison and community representatives helped to forge a robust and sustained partnership between them to improve student outcomes. This Title I school, surrounded by affluent communities in Westchester County, New York, attained dramatic academic growth as a result of becoming a full-service community school from 1996 to 2009, despite its challenges serving large numbers of low-income, Latino, and English language learners.

At times throughout the book, we have also included brief personal narratives in order to convey our individual experiences and perspectives in ways we hope will serve to inspire others to move forward with their own plans to create community schools. Finally, we hope to convey to our readers the tremendous opportunity that community schools represent for transforming both a conceptual model of child development and theory of how an educational ecosystem operates, into a variety of programs, services, and practices that will ultimately serve to benefit the whole child and all members of the school community.

UNDERSTANDING WHOLE CHILD EDUCATION AND THE EDUCATIONAL ECOSYSTEM OF CHILDREN'S GROWTH AND DEVELOPMENT: A VITAL COROLLARY TO IMPROVING STUDENT ACHIEVEMENT

Experiences in community schools have taught us how Human Ecology Theory plays an essential role in understanding that student achievement is not merely an outcome of what happens in school or one's genetic disposition, but it includes what can be described as an "educational ecosystem" consisting of a series of outside influences with the child as its center of impact. In this book, a framework for understanding how some schools have managed to succeed when so many others have failed is offered through a discussion of Human Ecology Theory, also known as Ecological Systems Theory, developed by Urie Bronfenbrenner (1979).

"Heavily influenced by the theories of Vygotsky, Bronfenbrenner viewed children's development as occurring within a system of relationships that shape their environment" (Martin, Fergus, and Noguera, 2010, 97). Bronfenbrenner described the ways in which complex "layers" of environment interact, and in his work he outlined four types of nested environmental systems that influence a child's development:

1. The Microsystem of social relationships includes settings that have direct and immediate influences upon the child (for example, the family, classroom, or peer group) participating directly in them.
2. The Mesosystem creates a local context and sets the parameters under which the Microsystems are operative and interconnected (for example, home-school, family-neighborhood) with the child still an active participant in these environments.
3. The Exosystem refers to those interconnected settings of power that can influence human development indirectly but in which the child does not actually participate. Bronfenbrenner (1979, page 255) defines settings of power as those in which the participants control the allocation of resources and make decisions affecting what happens in other settings (for example, school districts, state education departments, and town planning boards).
4. At the outermost layer is the Macrosystem, which represents the larger or overarching cultural and political context that also impacts child development, even if their influences are the most indirect (for example, laws, demographic patterns, and economic and ideological trends).

The underlying assumption of an "educational ecosystem" is that any of these environmental layers will positively or adversely impact the child's growth and development as they directly or indirectly interact with one another. This theoretical framework can readily be applied to creating dynamic and responsive educational institutions in which schools function as hubs for their communities, harnessing and integrating resources at all levels with an emphasis on partnership with the home and community organizations in order to improve student outcomes.

The concept of an "educational ecosystem" provides a broader framework for planning school reform initiatives and involves an approach to education that embraces the "whole child," taking into account the growing body of conceptual knowledge and research from the fields of education, sociology, psychology, and neuropsychology, all of which underscores the complex nature of children's growth and learning. This book proposes that providing caring and healthy environmental systems for children within and outside of school is conducive to supporting Whole Child Education and acts as a vital corollary to improving student achievement.

Adapted from Maslow's theory concerned with the hierarchy of human needs (Maslow, 1962), Whole Child Education (see figure 1.1) is defined here in terms of five developmental domains including children's physical, social, emotional, ethical, and intellectual development (Ferrara and Santiago, 2007). From our various vantage points as practitioners, we have witnessed how barriers to normal physical, social-emotional, and ethical development (universal virtues commonly associated with "good" character) often hinder students' abilities to fulfill their intellectual potential and experience success in school.

For poor students, we have found that these barriers frequently include a lack of access to good nutrition, comprehensive health care, adequate housing, and a childhood and adolescence free from the stresses of growing up in poverty. Similarly, we have witnessed—and research supports this notion— how lack of access to learning opportunities outside of school also hampers children's development (Clark, 1988; Carnegie Council on Adolescent Development, 1992).

Removing barriers and expanding opportunities for learning and healthy development are central to the community schools' strategy. Over the years, our respective roles in community schools have shown us the power of this reform effort in removing such barriers and in nurturing the development of the whole child. Whole Child Education is thus represented in this book (figure 1.1) by those instructional practices, service delivery models, and programs that work in tandem with one another so easily within the context of community schools to address the overall developmental needs of children and youth.

With a narrow focus on improving test scores at the state and federal levels, schools—in our view—have failed to meet the needs of the whole child. Efforts to improve the academic performance of children, particularly those living in poverty, would be better served by creating schools that are truly responsive to the needs we have identified within our working definition of Whole Child Education. Leadership in this kind of a school setting will require drawing from one's own personal experiences facing similar challenges growing up or thinking "out of the box" for those having never experienced poverty or living under conditions of extreme duress.

THE PRINCIPAL'S PERSPECTIVE: STUDENT ACHIEVEMENT IS MORE THAN THE SUM TOTAL OF WHAT HAPPENS IN THE CLASSROOM

When appointed in 1996 to be the principal to the Thomas Edison Elementary School located in the village of Port Chester, I was surprised to find myself

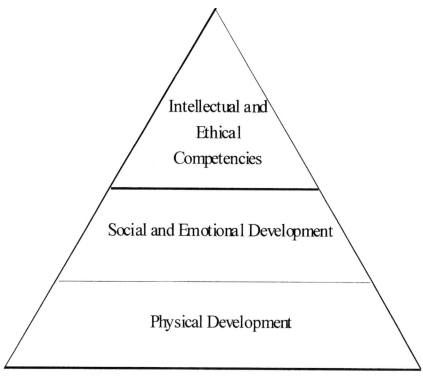

Figure 1.1. A Working Definition of Whole Child Education

in a Title I school much like those in the poorest inner-city neighborhoods in which I had once served as a teacher. Meetings and conversations with children, parents, teachers, and community representatives confirmed my own first impressions that this school indeed had an "urban profile" with a 94 percent minority population of black and Hispanic students living in poverty, the overwhelming majority of which were Hispanic immigrants of both documented and undocumented status.

My tenure as principal began with reflecting upon my own experiences as a student in the public schools of Spanish Harlem and the support that I had received during high school and later in college as part of President Johnson's "Great Society" initiative in which comprehensive funding for education was deemed to be the answer to eliminating poverty. In my own case, this proved to be true, and I can still recall the networking assistance and financial help I received from the college I attended, which had established a special program for opening its Ivy League doors to poor, minority students who had excelled in their high schools.

The level of support necessary for success in my first year of college was particularly evident during the mass transit strike in New York City in the early 1970s when the college most graciously offered me cab fare to get to class because they recognized that my parents would be unable to afford this expense, not owning a car or even being able to drive. Later, as a doctoral research fellow examining school reform, I made the connection between my own experiences, the organization of schools, and academic performance, gaining a clear understanding that student achievement is more than the sum total of what happens in the classroom.

COMMUNITY SCHOOLS DEFINED

Former St. Paul (Minnesota) schools superintendent Patricia Harvey has defined community schools as "a strategy for organizing the resources of the community around student success." The Coalition for Community Schools, a national consortium of advocates and practitioners, established a fieldwide consensus definition that is totally consistent with Harvey's conceptualization:

> A community school is both a place and a set of partnerships between the school and other community resources. Its integrated focus on academics, services, supports and opportunities leads to improved student learning, stronger families and healthier communities. Schools become the centers of the community and are open to everyone—all day, every day, evenings and weekends. (Blank et al., 2003)

There are several nationally recognized models of community schools, all of which fit these definitions: the Beacon schools in New York and several other cities; Bridges to Success, through which local United Ways partner with public schools to coordinate additional supports and services; Communities in Schools, a national organization that adds human and financial resources in over two thousand schools across the country; Schools of the 21st Century, a model developed by Yale University educators that integrates early childhood experiences into elementary education; the university-assisted model created by the Center for Community Partnerships at the University of Pennsylvania; and others.

All of the aforementioned models—and many local districts that have taken the community schools strategy to scale—have worked together through the Coalition for Community Schools to realize the collective vision of "every school a community school."

THE HISTORY AND
BACKGROUND OF COMMUNITY SCHOOLS

Historian John S. Rogers argues that the present "generation" of community schools is really the fourth iteration of this sound idea—the first having been created by John Dewey, Jane Addams, and other leaders of the Progressive era, followed by advances in the 1930s and again in the 1960s (Rogers, 1998). Joy Dryfoos (1998) cites, in particular, the influence of the settlement house movement of the late 1800s as the precursor to today's full-service community school with its emphasis on the role of neighborhood institutions in bringing about social and educational reforms for poor families, especially the waves of immigrants coming to the United States during the late nineteenth century and over the course of the twentieth century.

These early reform efforts—which included programs and services to help ensure positive youth development, good physical and mental health, and family and community well-being—would later evolve into what Dryfoos characterized as "settlement houses in schools," with a shift of programs and services to the school site.

The Children's Aid Society provides an illustrative example of the shift or colocation of services at the school when it successfully launched its own campaign in 1992 to support children and families living in poverty within the Washington Heights area. In doing so, this nonprofit organization partnered with the New York City public schools, an institution of higher learning, and charitable organizations to implement their model of a community school (Children's Aid Society, 2001).

In order to minimize the loss of instructional time and to situate the school context as the site for addressing the five developmental domains of children we have identified as the basic tenets of the community school (physical, social, emotional, ethical, and intellectual), the Children's Aid Society continued and expanded the practice of placing as many of its supports and services as possible within the school and integrating these services with each school's core instructional program.

The approach taken by the Children's Aid Society in implementing their community schools responded directly to one of the major challenges raised in a historical analysis by Rogers (1998), in which he observed that the community schools strategy had failed to take hold as a permanent reform model in large part because the earlier iterations were not adequately aligned with the core mission of the schools.

BUILDING ORGANIZATIONAL
CAPACITY THROUGH PARTNERSHIP

The thoughtfully designed community school not only responds to the needs of students and families but is also the catalyst for community renewal and capacity building at various levels. Stone (2001) and Noguera (2003), for example, described the notion of building "civic capacity" in driving school reform and the need for private and public organizations and institutions, not necessarily linked to education, to actively support schools by bringing the resources they control to bear on the goal of educating students.

Building civic capacity is particularly suited to a shift from traditional schooling, in which meeting the needs of the student population remains solely in the hands of school personnel, to community schools as a strategy that uses the resources of the community to nurture all aspects of child development to ensure that academic success is likely.

The ability of outside organizations to enhance their civic capacity in the community school is made possible through partnership. Community schools enable a range of outside organizations, from local arts councils to health providers, to redefine or actualize their outreach missions by sharing their resources with the school. Furthermore, in extending their partnerships to include local colleges and universities these institutions of higher learning gain a greater capacity to directly support the schools while simultaneously expanding their practical knowledge about Whole Child Education.

At the Thomas Edison Elementary School, a Professional Development School (PDS) partnership with Manhattanville College was successfully launched as one of its community school initiatives. This PDS partnership best demonstrates the "capacity building" described by Noguera in that it enabled the college to improve its outcomes for their teacher candidates while simultaneously transforming Edison into a laboratory of learning. The partnership, comfortably nested in a community school setting, easily allowed preservice, beginning, and experienced teachers to enhance their knowledge about comprehensive and integrated approaches to educating the whole child through their collaborations with a myriad of professionals.

THE GROWTH OF EDISON'S
FIVE STRATEGIC PARTNERSHIPS

Edison initiated its first partnership in 1998 in response to the urgent need for childcare expressed by parents. This partnership involved SER (the organization's name representing the words services, education, and resources) of Westchester, Inc., a local affiliate of a national organization whose mission was to support the progress of Hispanics through education and employment opportunities. Through a small corporate grant to this partner organization, the school was able to provide after-school homework help and remedial instruction for approximately thirty students in grades three through five.

Two years later, SER received a larger grant from the state to expand after-school programming to approximately 150 students from kindergarten through fifth grade, supplementing homework help with enrichment offerings, small group instruction, and individual tutoring.

From 1996 to 2009, Edison grew to maintain five "strategic" partnerships nurtured in response to the needs of students and families. In addition to the SER after-school program, which represented the first such partnership, a school-based health center was made possible through federal funding obtained by the area's congressional representative, Nita Lowey, and by the Open Door Family Medical Centers, Inc. (often referred to as Open Door), a local nonprofit medical organization.

The initiation of a school-based health center proved to be a vital component of Edison's community school design. This component served to support the health and wellness of Edison students with ancillary benefits extended to parents and staff. Efforts of the school-based health center were complemented by a third partnership with the Guidance Center, a mental health organization in Westchester County that provided therapeutic counseling at the school for emotionally at-risk students, along with secondary or colateral support for their families.

A fourth partnership gave parents the opportunity to continue their own learning through the many adult education courses offered at the school site during the evenings by the state's Board of Cooperative Educational Services (BOCES). Finally, a unique aspect of the Thomas Edison community school strategy, since its inception, was its consistent emphasis on teacher engagement and professional development made possible through the school's fifth partnership with the School of Education at Manhattanville College. The result of all of Edison's partnerships was to jointly create a full-service community school that delivered services not only to children but also to an entire school community.

THE PERSPECTIVE OF THE DIRECTOR OF THE NATIONAL CENTER FOR COMMUNITY SCHOOLS: COMMUNITY SCHOOLS AS A "NOT ONE SIZE FITS ALL" REFORM STRATEGY

From a national perspective, the partnerships initiated by the Thomas Edison Elementary School represent a very solid approach that other schools can emulate. Edison determined what kinds of partners it needed, making careful

*selections that would respond to the highest priority needs identified through
an examination of existing and new data.*

*Conducting a systematic need and resource assessment is essential to the
development of an effective community school. In addition to Edison's approach—in which the school selects and organizes an array of responsive
community resources—other schools have made the decision to partner with a
lead agency that serves as both a provider and broker of services, carrying out
many of the coordinating roles that the Edison team decided to play on its own.*

*For example, the Children's Aid Society plays that lead agency role in
twenty-two schools in New York City. The Chicago Community Schools initiative and the SUN (Schools Uniting Neighborhoods) schools in Portland,
Oregon (two of the country's largest and most mature community school efforts) also use a lead agency model.*

*Because community schools do not represent a "one size fits all" ap-
proach, programs and services, leadership infrastructures, partnerships,
funding, and the level of colocation of services will vary depending upon
need and feasibility; however, the essential ingredient in all of these models,
including Edison, is the hiring of a community school director who must work
closely with the school's principal to coordinate the multiple community resources and to integrate them into the school's core instructional program.*

The illustration in figure 1.2 depicts Edison's community school design
as a "one-stop" location in which two levels of support were provided. The
"one-stop family resource component" allowed children and families to access a variety of resources, including counseling assistance, case management
services, parent education programs, and health and wellness programs. The
"one-stop student support component" provided students with social skills development, tutorial assistance, homework assistance, sports and recreational
activities, and enrichment experiences through literacy-related initiatives (for
example, book clubs and a variety of student publications) and the arts.

In Edison's design, both levels of support were intended to improve teaching and learning by strengthening the overall development of its students.
Figure 1.2 thus provides a useful Whole Child Education framework for the
design of programs and services within a community school.

CHAPTER SUMMARY

This chapter describes how children have become lost in our public schools
as a result of school reform efforts narrowly focused on improving test scores.
As advocates on their behalf, we urge educators and policymakers to reevalu-
ate these reform efforts in order to consider the needs of the whole child and

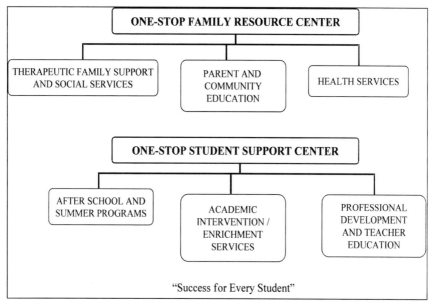

Figure 1.2.   Thomas Edison, Full-Service Community School Model (Ferrara and Santiago, 2007)

those layers of the entire "educational ecosystem" that have the potential to ameliorate the impact of poverty on student achievement.

A framework is introduced for implementing Whole Child Education drawing upon the theories of Maslow and Bronfenbrenner, and school reform is conceptualized in terms of strategically planning for the design of a healthy "educational ecosystem" best exemplified in the community school. The potential of community schools to improve student achievement is extended to include facilitating the work of teachers, supporting families, and actualizing the mission and civic capacity of partner agencies. In succeeding chapters, we provide a road map for developing a community school based upon more than a decade's worth of experience at Edison and the collective wisdom and experiences of the authors.

Chapter Two

The Core of Professional Competencies and Knowledge Essential to the Effective Implementation of a Community School

In developing the road map to becoming a community school, the five developmental domains of children described in chapter 1 constitute the nonnegotiable tenets of this approach. It is, therefore, critically important that every community school address the physical, social, emotional, ethical, and intellectual growth of children within its design framework.

When planning for community schools, it is less important to discuss whether to replicate all or part of the strategies described in this book or to insist upon the colocation of all programs and services at the school site than it is to focus on a design that will deliver all programs and services in a manner that ensures quality student and community engagement and that establishes the conditions needed for learning and healthy development to take place.

The term *full-service community school*, as described in this book and in relation to descriptions about the Thomas Edison Elementary School, implies the integration of a wide variety of programs and services at the school site; however, a community school may not necessarily be able to house all of these programs and services. Turning one's vision of a community school into a reality thus requires an incremental and customized approach that is driven by an understanding of student and family needs and takes into account the availability of space, personnel, and funding.

There are community schools across the country that operate some of their partnerships outside of the building, as in the example of those unable to house a school-based health center and who have opted instead to establish a partnership with a neighborhood health care facility or hospital that allows students to routinely access their resources, being escorted by their parents or other adult chaperone before, during, and after the school day.

As another example, the Children's Aid Society operates several models, including five full-service community schools that include on-site health and mental health centers as well as a school-linked model that involves offering health, mental health, and early childhood services at a centrally located neighborhood center that has explicit links to five nearby public schools. Another central tenet of community schools is responding to documented needs by increasing access to supports, services, and opportunities. The flexibility of the strategy revolves around the fact that there are often multiple ways to respond to these documented needs.

Preparing for implementation requires establishing a new core of professional competencies and knowledge essential for training administrators, teachers, and those engaged in partnership with the school. As part of chapter 2, we introduce a new set of skills and conceptual knowledge for all serving in leadership roles as they consider shifting the organization of their own schools to reflect the philosophy and practices characteristic of the community school.

The core competencies articulated convey a leadership infrastructure that allows for participatory leadership at all levels of the school's organization and enables its community partners to move easily and fluidly across the boundaries of their respective organizations, with everyone involved learning to accept and respect each other's areas of expertise.

Chapter 2 also provides a valuable framework for developing a Strategic Action Plan to design and evaluate the array of programs, services, and practices implemented as part of the community school. Finally, this chapter describes how community school initiatives can be supported by combining sources of funding available to the school district with outside grants, by establishing reasonable fees for the services provided, and through the exchange of in-kind services.

Designing a community school requires substantive changes in how schools are typically organized and the ways in which they operate. In planning for successful implementation, one should always bear in mind that often failures in school reform have resulted from a lack of fidelity to the conceptual, philosophical, and pedagogical underpinnings intended to fundamentally change the way schools operate and the behaviors of the professionals who work within them (Fullan, 2007).

The chart presented in table 2.1 details the core competencies and knowledge developed by Edison to plan and sustain its own model of a community school. The set of skills and knowledge depicted here will undoubtedly play an important role in facilitating the changes necessary for those interested in starting their own community school with fidelity to the basic underpinnings of how effective community schools best operate.

The decision to implement a community school typically begins in one of several ways: from the "top down" as a district initiative; from the "bot-

Table 2.1. The Core Competencies and Knowledge for Designing and Implementing the Community School

Core Competencies: Skills Needed	Related Core Knowledge: What You Need to Know
1. Engaging stakeholders in the development of a shared vision and the design of a community school based upon a conceptual model of child development and the nonnegotiable tenets of Whole Child Education.	• Human Ecology Theory and its relevance to the design of school programs and services that respond to the documented needs of children and families. • The nonnegotiable tenets of Whole Child Education and their application to programs and services that help ensure students are healthy, safe, engaged, supported, and challenged (ASCD, 2007).
2. Developing a Strategic Action Plan for designing and implementing a community school, including the use of data to inform decision making and evaluate outcomes.	• The process of conducting needs assessments that use academic and nonacademic data from multiple sources. • The components of a Strategic Action Plan that involves community partners and their resources in actively supporting the whole child with measurable academic and nonacademic outcomes for students, families, and other key stakeholders.
3. Managing school change and facilitating productive group work.	• Strategies for building consensus, commitment, and teamwork with school personnel and community partners.
4. Identifying, allocating, and combining a variety of resources for funding the community school.	• District, state, and federal funding sources that can be used to support programs and services. • Knowledge about flexible and innovative funding sources. • Grant writing and fund-raising to begin, enhance, or sustain community school programming. • Sustainability strategies that go beyond (but include) fund-raising.
5. Supporting leadership that crosses boundaries in the community school.	• Multileveled leadership and its implications for community school governance, management, program implementation, and long-term sustainability.

tom up" as a school-based initiative; or ideally from a "joint initiative" in which both the school and district concurrently pursue the idea and work collaboratively to seamlessly comingle their resources on behalf of children and families. Regardless of how the decision is made to implement this approach to schooling, it is absolutely necessary to give thoughtful and detailed consideration to the core competencies outlined. The danger of not doing so is to allow community partners to merely exist as tenants within the school building without true collaboration.

When a school does effectively make use of these core competencies, it is not only transformed into a "hub" of programs and services for the community but also becomes an innovative training ground for those entering the human services professions (teachers, social workers, psychologists, guidance counselors, and health practitioners) and a vehicle for turning Whole Child Education into a reality. The core competencies and knowledge described ensure that, despite which approach is used to initiate change in becoming a community school (top down, bottom up, or jointly initiated), this change is conceptualized in terms of the integration of theory, research, and practice.

CORE COMPETENCY #1:
DESIGNING A VISIONARY COMMUNITY SCHOOL

The Thomas Edison Elementary School used the "bottom up" approach when deciding to become a full-service community school and, in getting started, key stakeholders were identified and engaged as part of the school's initial planning team, which would later become its Community School Advisory Board. It is also important to note the pivotal role played by district leadership in this planning process and in sustaining community school initiatives over the years by facilitating the school's access to a variety of funding sources, including, for example, part of its Title I and Drug and Violence Prevention allocations.

While most school improvement planning teams are comprised entirely of school/district personnel and parents, Edison created a broad leadership infrastructure that included a number of community organizations that would bring much-needed resources to the school beyond what the district was able to provide. From discussions with these internal and external stakeholders, what emerged were a number of concerns that became priorities in putting together a Strategic Action Plan for school improvement.

Although initially focused upon improving academic achievement, stakeholders were also encouraged to envision their children as adults and to describe what personal attributes they wished for them to develop as they grew into adulthood. These visioning activities, conducted in both workshop and discussion group formats, were vital to the process of laying the foundation for the development of a Strategic Action Plan with goals beyond student achievement and consistent with the design of a community school committed to the education of the whole child.

The Strategic Action Plan developed by Edison's planning team would become the design blueprint from which to reframe existing programs and build new ones.

It is our recommendation that planning for the implementation of a community school begin with the creation of a leadership infrastructure that not only represents staff and parents but also represents key partners from within the community, securing the support of district leadership as well. With representative leadership in place and engaged, the process of developing an organizational mission statement ensues, with this process being as important as the development of the plan itself.

In addition to the goal of achieving academic success, both the planning team and members of the entire Edison community also wanted the school to nurture qualities of good character and citizenship in their children and to help them overcome the challenges of poverty that hinder socioeconomic advancement. The planning process progressed from "envisioning the possibilities of what could be" to the development of a mission statement aligned to a vision of schooling that would uphold the rigor of state standards for learning while demonstrating compassion and service to children and families.

The ideas expressed in the mission statement below were generated with stakeholders within and external to the building. These ideas were then captured in writing and translated into Spanish for Edison's multiethnic Hispanic population, becoming the catalyst for the design of all school programs, practices, and services. This mission statement reflected the growing knowledge and commitment of Edison families to its model of school-linked services as a community school.

Edison's Community School Mission Statement

At the Thomas Edison Elementary School, children's physical, social, emotional, ethical, and intellectual development are central to all school initiatives. We believe that improving the quality of life within the community and strengthening community connections have a positive impact on our children's growth and learning. Our full-service community school provides services to students in a comprehensive manner. It also strengthens the network of relationships between the child's home, school, and community, enabling our students to come to school ready to learn and experience academic success.

CORE COMPETENCY #2:
DEVELOPING A STRATEGIC ACTION PLAN
THAT USES DATA TO INFORM DECISION MAKING

Schools with high levels of poverty, significant numbers of non-English-speaking families, and limited levels of literacy (even in the student's primary language) require that school planning teams assess the needs of children in ways that will provide much-needed insights about their lives at home, at school, and even within their neighborhoods. Typical school improvement efforts are directed toward planning academic or behavioral interventions with little consideration for the complex but vital network of environmental systems that interact with one another, as described in chapter 1, to influence child development and ultimately student achievement.

Collecting information about life outside of school, however, can often be difficult for school personnel and demands creativity in mining multiple sources of information so that different perspectives can form the complete picture.

THE PRINCIPAL'S PERSPECTIVE:
GATHERING MEANINGFUL DATA

As a principal, I always looked at students' needs from an ecological perspective, considering all aspects of child development and environments for learning in planning for school improvement with our planning team. Outcomes from meetings, surveys, and focus groups involving teachers, parents, students, and community representatives revealed the complexity of students' lives. Minutes of these meetings were used to extract common themes, helping us to identify factors, within and outside of school, that were directly or indirectly impacting upon student learning.

I remember the frustration of sending out written survey forms that were often not returned. Our partnership with Open Door, then in the process of preparing to open the district's first school-based health center in our building, allowed their staff to help us collect valuable information about the very limited access of our students to quality health care and to tease out the multiple layers of stress many families were experiencing as a result of immigration and living in conditions of extreme poverty.

Instead of survey forms, we opted for bilingually conducted face-to-face interviews whenever we had a captive audience throughout the year, such as during our kindergarten orientation, the registration of new entrants, Open House activities at the beginning of the school year, and at almost every PTA or schoolwide function. What we learned was that every meeting with a parent or family member was an opportunity to get or share information.

We also learned the value of uncovering and analyzing existing in-house data that was already available but often overlooked, including attendance at important school functions such as parent conferences and curriculum orientation nights. Finally and perhaps most importantly, we learned that parents had to feel safe when answering any of our questions, particularly with regard to overcoming their fears about being reported to immigration authorities or in speaking openly about their needs and concerns.

The variety of ways in which the needs of families were assessed proved to be particularly effective in addressing the needs of our poor, working, and preliterate parents, many of whom were otherwise unable to communicate their concerns to school personnel. When these parental concerns were correlated with our own observations, we concluded that children's intellectual growth and learning were significantly influenced by their physical, social, and emotional development during their formative years.

COMPONENTS OF THE COMMUNITY SCHOOL STRATEGIC ACTION PLAN

The preceding discussion about the importance of taking an extensive and sometimes inventive approach to conducting needs assessments is essential to the strategic planning process. The Strategic Action Plan, which includes the components described below, should thus focus on meeting the documented needs of the whole child in a community school setting.

- Needs Assessments: In establishing a community school, needs assessments must focus on the concerns of students and their families, as well as on the learning that takes place within and beyond the classroom. Therefore, it is important to analyze multiple sources of information (in addition to student achievement data) for common themes and trends in order to gain a deeper understanding of both the challenging and enabling factors behind student achievement. Included in a needs assessment should be the perspectives of both internal and external stakeholders to the school, as they represent significant influences within the educational ecosystem.
- Mission Statement: A mission statement for a community school requires that all aspects of the overall developmental growth of children and youth be valued and recognized as an important part of improving student achievement. Therefore, the mission statement should reflect the basic tenets of Whole Child Education with student success more broadly defined

in terms of achieving intellectual, ethical, and social competency, along
with good physical and mental health.

- Strategic Goals: In creating the Strategic Action Plan for a community
  school, a limited number of achievable and generally stated outcomes or
  goals are prioritized that reflect the school's mission statement and the
  needs of children, families, and school staff with a specified time frame for
  achieving them.
- Strategic Objectives, Activities, and Time Lines: Strategic objectives represent the specific actions to be taken and are correlated to one or more
  goals of the Strategic Action Plan. Objectives should be measurable and not
  limited to student achievement results as measured by standardized tests.
  Although student achievement is critical, the strategic objectives for the
  implementation of a community school should also measure the impact of
  programs and services on children's physical, social-emotional, and more
  broadly defined intellectual outcomes using both quantitative and qualitative data. These objectives should be revisited and updated annually by
  those implementing the plan.
- Evaluation: Evaluation measures should be both formative and summative in nature. Formative measures, correlated to short-term objectives, are
  those typically used to inform decision making along the way and, as part
  of a Strategic Action Plan, include a brief explanation of how each objective will be measured after a specified period of time as the benchmark used
  to signify that progress has been achieved. Summative or more long-term
  measures typically span a three-year period for data collection and analysis
  and are particularly helpful in assessing the overall effectiveness of the
  Strategic Action Plan.

As part of the community school strategy, the responsibilities for evaluation are shared with community partners and include multiple indicators of
success across a range of the developmental domains of children. In addition
to measuring changes in student knowledge, skills, attitudes, and behaviors,
evaluation strategies should similarly determine the impact of community
school initiatives on parents and teachers (for example, such as increases in
parental involvement and teacher skills and knowledge).

Community schools have the advantage of being able to identify other indicators of success, including, for example, the BMI (Body Mass Index) of students, which could be tracked over a period of time to determine the impact
of health and wellness initiatives. Evaluation measures that are focused on
achieving both academic and nonacademic outcomes are vital to the process
of continuous improvement within the community school.

What distinguishes the Strategic Action Plan for the community school
from all others is that the programs and services offered must be both com-

prehensive and integrated with one another, and they should include the sharing of resources in ways that transcend the boundaries in which traditional schools and community organizations generally operate. In all cases, specific memoranda of understanding must follow in order to define any newly created positions, duties, fiscal responsibilities, and liabilities that have been carved out for participating organizations.

Finally, the plan must also include a description of any relevant curricular and instructional undertakings, significant professional development initiatives, related pupil personnel activities, and services offered on-site or as off-site extensions for children, their families, and staff.

Given that people, times, and circumstances change, Strategic Action Plans document the work to be carried out in a dynamic educational ecosystem and must therefore be revisited periodically to successfully respond to these changes. For this reason, it had always been the practice of the Thomas Edison Elementary School to write its Strategic Action Plan for a three-year period and to review it annually. Excerpts are offered from two of these plans, the first of which was written in 1996 when the seeds for the community school were first germinated (see table 2.2), and the second, developed in 1999 and presented in table 2.3, documents the school's progress three years later.

Excerpts include self-description narratives that typically appear as part of the strategic action plan's introduction. These excerpts clearly illustrate how the planning team intentionally mapped out a journey to respond to changes in the school facility, student demographics, staff characteristics, and to the emergence of the Learning Standards movement with its corresponding changes in student and school accountability.

Also depicted in tables 2.2 and 2.3 are several of the plans' goals and objectives provided to give the reader important historical insights about the school and its early and ongoing commitment to forming partnerships with parents and the community for the purposes of school improvement. The evaluation processes used to determine the effectiveness of the community school Strategic Action Plan will be discussed later as part of chapter 4.

In addition to reflecting Edison's evolution as a community school, a comparison of the self-description narratives, goals, and objectives contained in each of the plan excerpts in tables 2.2 and 2.3 reflects the support, technical assistance, and professional development about community schools and the strategic planning process offered to the principal, teachers, parent representatives, and partners by such helpful organizations as the Coalition for Community Schools, the Children's Aid Society of New York, SER Jobs for Progress National, Inc., the Collaborative for Integrated School Services at Harvard University, the Westchester Children's Association, and Joy Dryfoos, a well-known expert in the field.

Table 2.2. Edison School Strategic Action Plan, 1996 to 1997

Edison School Strategic Action Plan: 1996 to 1997 School Self-Description Narrative

The Edison School is located in the village of Port Chester and presently has a population of 324 students in kindergarten through fourth grade. The school is a multistory facility that is more than one hundred years old. Recent construction has brought to fruition a dream, shared by both the school and its surrounding community, to have a playground in the back of the building where a vacant lot once stood.

Staff members remain committed to a vision of Edison as a nurturing place where children are expected to reach their full potential. To realize this vision, teachers have participated in professional development activities in order to extend their knowledge regarding the ways in which to both stimulate and challenge learners from diverse backgrounds. Over the next three years, the school will continue to focus on raising levels of student achievement by instituting organizational changes and establishing a variety of avenues for collaboration with the community at large.

1996 Strategic Action Plan Goals	*Corresponding Goal Objectives*
Goal #1. Edison will raise levels of student achievement by providing increased opportunities for language and literacy development in all classrooms. To implement this goal we intend to increase the ability of children to think critically and to make effective use of oral and written language across the content areas.	1a. Over the next three years, all classroom teachers will receive training on the new assessments and standards-based learning, particularly in the area of English Language Arts. At least 90 percent of the teachers observed by the school or district administrators will be rated as satisfactory or better in relation to implementing these new learning standards on their yearly evaluations. 1b. A 10 percent growth measure criterion will be established for third grade, assessed by the state in ELA each year, with the goal of attaining and sustaining the 90 percent passing rate established by the New York State Education Department in the next three years.
Goal #2. Edison will offer greater opportunities for parent and larger community involvement. Broader community involvement will not only enrich our instructional programs but also help Edison families secure the resources they will need to improve the quality of their lives.	2a. Edison will increase (and reshape when necessary) the number of schoolwide activities designed to promote positive interactions and greater participation among all members of the Edison school community each year over the next three years. 2b. Edison will increase the number of families attending schoolwide activities each year by 10 percent over the next three years with teacher and parent reporting information about the 1995–1996 school year serving as the baseline for data collection. 2c. Edison will increase the number of parents on committees sponsored by the PTA and School Improvement Team by 10 percent each year over the next three years with the 1995–1996 school year serving as the baseline for data collection. 2d. Edison will increase the number of partnerships with community agencies and the corporate sector each year over the next three years.

Table 2.3. Edison School Strategic Action Plan, 1998 to 1999

Edison School Strategic Action Plan: 1998 to 1999 School Self-Description Narrative

Recent renovations have transformed Edison's once unfinished basement into the Edison School Community Services and Technology Explorations Center. This center (funded through the district, SER National Jobs for Progress, and other partner organizations) has served as the focal point for staff development, parent education, community outreach, and computer instruction for adults and children. As a result of Edison's unique and innovative ability to work collaboratively with partner organizations, it has been identified as one of four full-service community school demonstration sites across the country.

Over the next three years, Edison School will continue to focus on raising levels of student achievement commensurate with the rigorous requirements established by the new standards for learning in the areas of English Language Arts and math, science, social studies, and technology. In addition, district construction/renovation plans will add three new classrooms to Edison, replace the existing library and cafeteria with more modern facilities, and repair the building exterior. As a result, Edison is slated to become a K–5 elementary school with approximately 425 students in September 2002.

1999 Strategic Action Goals	Corresponding Goal Objectives
Goal #1. To raise levels of student achievement by providing increased opportunities for language and literacy development in all classrooms. To implement this goal, we intend to increase the ability of children to demonstrate their understanding of written and oral text beyond the literal level through well-organized and thoughtful writing and effective use of language mechanics (based on NYS Learning Standards 1999).	1a. Over the next three years, all Edison teachers will receive training on implementing Balanced Literacy instruction within their classrooms. At least 90 percent of the teachers observed by school and/or district administrators will be rated satisfactory or better yearly in implementing the following components of Balanced Literacy instruction: leveling reading materials, creating literacy centers, conducting shared reading/writing activities, conducting guided reading/writing activities, conducting independent/ writing activities, implementing buddy activities, facilitating writing across the curriculum, using authentic and informal assessments to inform instruction, and generating assessment rubrics with students to jointly evaluate their work.
	1b. Edison will increase the percentage of fourth grade students achieving a passing score on new standards-based assessments in ELA from 19 percent in year 1 of the plan to 39 percent during the second year of the plan's implementation. The projected breakdown of students achieving a passing score during the third year of the plan will be 60 percent at level 3 and 20 percent at level 4 (80 percent passing in total); however, the actual number of students scoring at these levels will also be influenced by any new students admitted to the fourth grade during the school year.

Table 2.3. (continued)

Goal #2. Edison will offer greater opportunities for parent and larger community involvement. Broader community involvement will not only enrich our instructional programs but also help Edison families secure the resources they will need to improve the quality of their lives and the readiness of their children to learn and experience success in school.	2a. Edison will increase the number of families attending schoolwide activities, based upon the Developmental Studies Center–related publication titled At Home in Our Schools, by 10 percent each year over the next three years. The 1999–2000 school year will provide the baseline for data collection. 2b. Edison will have 80 percent of students and their parents or guardians in each class complete family engagement activities from the Developmental Studies Center publication titled Homeside Activities (Developmental Studies Center, 1995b), during the 1999–2000 school year. Participation will then increase to at least 90 percent of the school population in 2000–2001, the third year of plan implementation. 2c. Edison will increase the participation of its parents (especially Hispanic) serving on the Community School Advisory Board (formerly the School Improvement Team), PTA, or any other leadership committee within the school by 10 percent over the next three years with the 1998–1999 school year serving as the baseline for data collection. 2d. Edison will engage at least 50 percent of the parents or guardians in each class in PTA-sponsored events and activities by June 1999 and increase such participation by 10 percent each year thereafter until June 2001.

Most importantly, the strategic plan excerpts also provide documented evidence of the accomplishments of Edison's School Improvement Team (later to become the Community School Advisory Board) from 1996 to 1999. These accomplishments included the following:

- Articulating the importance of establishing school-linked services to support the overall developmental growth of students so that they are ready to benefit from academic instruction.
- Transforming Edison into a "one-stop location" that would allow students, their families, and the community at large to avail themselves of important services, thereby requiring the planning team to think creatively about the design and maximized use of school space and to plan for intentionally building relational trust across the school community (Bryk et al., 2010).
- Supporting parents in fulfilling their roles respective to their own children, providing opportunities for their direct involvement with the school's curriculum, and empowering them as members of the community school.
- Responding to forthcoming federal mandates in assessing student performance and in holding schools accountable under the No Child Left Behind legislation by implementing specific initiatives aimed at improving curriculum and instruction.
- Formalizing Edison's role as one of four community school demonstration sites throughout the country as a result of the advocacy efforts of congressional representatives Nita Lowey and Steny Hoyer.

CORE COMPETENCY #3: MANAGING SCHOOL CHANGE AND FACILITATING PRODUCTIVE GROUP WORK

The implementation of a community school not only requires managing school change but also engaging in team building in order to facilitate collaboration within and across participating organizations. Team building creates the essential element of relational trust (Bryk et al., 2010) that comes through friendly and supportive personal interactions, which in turn encourages the open exchange of ideas and the many "aha" moments that result in more informed planning and decision making. It also helps to generate commitment among those who will primarily be responsible for implementing the Strategic Action Plan.

Team building must take place at all levels of the planning and implementation process, including opportunities to build relationships among the school's planning team, at meetings involving the entire faculty with school partners, and at meetings with district-level representatives. These activities

should be fun, energizing, and encourage self-reflection for everyone involved. Although typically conducted at the start of the meeting, team-build-
ing activities can easily be conducted in the middle, either before or after a
break, or as part of the conclusion and wrap-up of such gatherings.

Just as team building helps to launch an effective meeting and attends to
one aspect of group dynamics, a well-run meeting must also closely attend to
additional "relational" elements concerned with building consensus, decision
making, and conflict resolution. Effective teamwork requires initial training, and this is especially true for community school planning teams who
must work with outside partners, as well as with their own faculty and staff.
This kind of training, which provides participants with a deeper understanding of the decision-making processes at their disposal, is available through
consultant support, outside organizations, and the many professional readings related to this topic (Mayer, 2004; London, 1995; Rahim, 2001; Rees,
2001; Snow and Phillips, 2007).

Community school planning teams should decide early on how they will
generally arrive at their decisions, taking into consideration the configuration
of stakeholders represented and how their voices will be heard. For example,
teams whose configuration consists of more school staff than community
partners may opt to provide greater parity in decision making by giving those
stakeholders with the most representation one collective vote so that others
may have an "equal say." Once the issue of parity is addressed, any one of the
following mechanisms for decision making may prove helpful:

- Decision by consensus: This mechanism for decision making usually entails the most amount of time as it requires that all group members agree to
  rule "in favor" or "not in favor" of a specific decision. However, the level
  of commitment to the decision rendered is usually greatest when this approach is used, and it is well worth the effort.
- Decision by majority: This mechanism for decision making is best known
  to the general public because of its similarity to the voting processes with
  which they are the most familiar. Simply put, it means that the majority will
  rule "in favor" or "not in favor" of a specific decision. Decisions made in
  this manner involve discussion but ultimately take less time and generate
  less commitment than when using a consensus model.
- Decision by informed authority: This mechanism also involves group discussion with recommendations turned over to an informed authority for a
  final decision. In this case, group members agree to defer to individuals
  outside of the group who have the appropriate level of knowledge or to a
  subcommittee within the group that has been charged with this task.

Another important "relational" element of group dynamics requires the understanding of how groups evolve and change over time and the role that conflict resolution plays in this process. This developmental process is evident during the team's first meetings when discussions are courteous but superficial in nature until the group has had the opportunity to have its first real exchange on substantive issues where there are different points of view. At this juncture, it is necessary for such teams to acknowledge that disagreement is a healthy part of the group's development and becomes problematic only when there are no strategies in place for resolving these conflicts.

To avoid hindering the group's progress, the team chairperson should act in a facilitative role early on by making each issue brought to the table an opportunity to engage the group in problem solving and establishing, together with them, explicit norms for listening and responding to one another respectfully and for allowing one's opinions and concerns to be shared. This can be readily accomplished by using the strategies designed for this purpose, described below:

- Creating a record of group discussion through public recording: Since many disagreements can occur over the accuracy of what was discussed and agreed upon at meetings, having a recorder take public minutes during meetings is critical to avoiding unnecessary conflict. These minutes should then be transcribed, reviewed, and approved at subsequent meetings in order to be disseminated among all stakeholders.
- Establishing and sticking to an agenda: Since group meetings can easily stray from substantive topics, agenda setting and time keeping are essential to maintaining the flow of the meeting. Agendas can be built with participants before the start or at the conclusion of a meeting, thereby helping to ensure that any unfinished business will not turn into an obstacle of insurmountable proportion. The assignment of a timekeeper should be made at the start of each meeting.
- Round-robin sharing: With the focus on active listening, this strategy allows for the open exchange of perspectives as each group member takes a turn expressing his or her views without interruption or comment from others.
- Partner discussions and building consensus by making the whole the sum of its parts: Difficulties in achieving consensus can often be a source of conflict for group members; however, this process may be made somewhat easier through discussion formats that move from small group to whole group. Such small-group discussions are first aimed at obtaining consensus within pairs and then work toward furthering consensus by incrementally

extending these discussions to include larger group configurations until the whole team is in agreement.

- Straw polling: This strategy allows the group facilitator and others present to quickly determine everyone's thoughts about an issue by surveying their responses. Unlike voting, group members simply indicate whether they would be "in favor" or "not in favor" of a particular outcome in order to frame and inform the overall discussion.

- The art of compromise: After the give and take of ideas, every conflict will require finding the middle ground or a position that everyone can live with happily or at least comfortably. The art of compromise therefore requires shifting the paradigm of one's thinking to arrive at inventive solutions that reflect a synthesis of group member perspectives and that have the potential to serve as a springboard in the design of new and exciting programs, services, and practices for the community school.

The Children's Aid Society (see Figure 7.1 beginning on page 112) has a useful self-assessment tool for examining the ways in which community schools develop their capacity to make effective decisions with regard to the following: the fundamentals of staffing, programs and services, management and governance, levels of integration, parent involvement, community involvement, and evaluation. Its rubric includes a description of the developmental stages in decision-making effectiveness (from exploring, to emerging, to maturing, and finally to excelling) and is extremely useful in assessing the developmental stages of planning teams, working committees, and of the leadership body of the community school charged with management and governance.

CORE COMPETENCY #4: IDENTIFYING, ALLOCATING, AND COMBINING A VARIETY OF RESOURCES FOR FUNDING THE COMMUNITY SCHOOL

As mentioned earlier in this chapter, funding the community school places school or district planning teams in the unique and sometimes overwhelming position of having to gain a more thorough understanding of fund-raising strategies. It is therefore recommended that teams further their knowledge of grant writing, generating service fees, bartering for the exchange of services, and using existing school and district allocations to support community school initiatives.

Programs, services, and positions can be carefully crafted to comply with federal or state funding streams, often referred to as "categorical funding" because of the specific compliance guidelines governing their expenditure.

Although a district's general funds may also be used to support community school initiatives and are not constrained by the guidelines of categorical funding, these funds may be constrained by the taxpayer who votes directly to approve the budget in small, noncity school districts throughout the country. Therefore, smaller districts with lean budgets may be less inclined to use the district's general funds, paid for through the tax levy process, to support community school programming.

The most practical methods for funding the community school may require that each program or service be funded on its own or in combination with other funding sources, with planning teams always keeping in mind the complete picture of how these programs and services will ultimately operate in coordination with one another. Planning teams also need to keep in mind that various funding sources and their cycles of funding are often contingent upon the economy and political climate of the time, reflecting Exosystem and Macrosystem considerations as described in the discussion of Human Ecology Theory in chapter 1.

The chart in table 2.4 shows examples of how categorical funding streams can be combined to support community school initiatives in a manner consistent with their funding guidelines. Fortunately, these guidelines typically require that related expenses be used to supplement and not supplant the school's regular instructional programs, thereby allowing enough flexibility to sustain community school initiatives. When used for the purpose of subsidizing such programs and services, federal or state "categorical funds" should always be developed around the nonnegotiable tenets of a community and its embrace of Whole Child Education.

Categorical funding streams are periodically reauthorized, revamped, or even eliminated; however, some federal monies—including Title I funding aimed at compensatory education in schools with high levels of poverty, Title III funding aimed at supporting programs for bilingual/ESL (English as a Second Language) students, and Title IV funding aimed at drug and violence prevention—have maintained a history of longevity and are used for illustrative purposes in table 2.4. The categorical funds used for illustrative purposes in the table emanate from the federal government but are often administered through state education departments and dispersed to the districts for expenditure.

The table clearly demonstrates how categorical funding can be applied to community school initiatives; planning teams should also find ways to be creative in obtaining additional resources, which may or may not necessarily entail a direct cost but rather the sharing of resources and expertise. Many of Edison's partnerships, for example, involved all parties in this kind of an exchange, including having the school principal and other faculty members

Table 2.4. Categorical Funding Sources

Categorical Funding Source	Funding Guidelines	Related Community School Initiatives Eligible for Funding	Allowable Expenditures
Title I (School allocations based on federal funding formula)	Compensatory education for schools with high levels of poverty	Family engagement programs for students with compensatory needs	Community School Coordinator
			Literacy and Family Outreach Coordinator
		After-school and summer programs for students with compensatory needs	Family Case Worker
			Reading and Academic Intervention Specialists working before, during, and after the school day
Title III (District allocations based on number of English Language Learners)	Support for English Language Learners (ELL)	Family engagement programs aimed at literacy support and acculturation for parents of ELL students	Counselors and Social Workers
		Bilingual or English as a Second Language (ESL) instructional programs held after school and during the summer	After-school and summer program personnel with appropriate certification
		Diversity training for community-based organizations in partnership with the school	Commercially prepared educational programs for adults and students
		Adult education programs for ELL students of school age	Curriculum development
Title IV (Allocations provided to all districts)	Drug and violence prevention	Character education programs	Program materials and supplies
	Early intervention	Mentoring programs	Consultant support
		Parenting education programs focusing on positive youth development	Parent training
		Preschool programs	Conference participation and professional development
			Subcontracts with partner agencies

regularly serve on various education advisory committees of its college partner and as guest speakers or panel presenters at its functions and events.

Grants can be particularly helpful in supporting large or smaller-scale projects. Several state funding streams, such as the New York State Advantage
After-School Program, have made available competitive grants for after-
school programming, allowing the Thomas Edison Elementary School to
have grown from once serving only thirty-five children after school through
corporate sponsorship to serving approximately 150 youngsters through state
grant funding.

On a smaller scale, charitable organizations or foundations can be used
to fund summer programs or even one-time purchases. In Edison's growth
as a community school, both federal funding and foundation grants have
been combined or used at different times, for example, to fund summer
programming. At a cost of about $25,000, Edison ran an all-day academic
and recreational program for nearly one hundred students by combining
both categorical and competitive grant dollars. The school's college partner
facilitated additional cost-saving measures by providing its preservice teacher
candidates with additional course credits to serve as program staff under the
guidance of an experienced teacher leader from the school.

Another project demonstrating the important role of smaller-scale grant
funding was "Edison's Closet." This project involved distributing clothing to
families in need within the neighborhood several times a year. Successfully
launched by a former Edison teacher and the community school caseworker
more than ten years ago, the project first received the financial support of the
Junior League of Westchester for the one-time purchase of clothing hangers,
racks, and storage bins that were used for this purpose on an ongoing basis.

Small grant sponsorship similar to the examples described can be attained
from sources at the local, state, and even national levels via foundations, philanthropic organizations, and even Teacher Centers. Teacher Centers, linked
to teacher unions and state departments of education, have been very helpful
in the past for providing competitive grant funding for small projects aiming
at professional growth and educational innovation.

Community schools across the country have found the 21st Century Community Learning Centers' funding to be a particularly relevant source, in part
because most states require that applicants demonstrate that they have crafted
viable school-community partnerships. The three mandatory components of
this funding source, which is allocated by the U.S. Department of Education
to the fifty state departments of education, are an excellent fit for community
schools as they involve after-school and summer programs that focus on
academic enrichment, positive youth development, and parent engagement.

As yet another strategy, community schools can also help schools access
noneducation dollars that can directly promote a student's success in school.

Medicaid is an excellent example of such a funding source. On their own, schools cannot access Medicaid funding. But if they partner with a licensed health provider that is authorized to bill Medicaid, the school can make these resources available to its students and, in some cases, families. The counseling services of the therapeutic social worker assigned to Edison through its mental health partner (The Guidance Center) were successfully obtained through this method.

The key to successful community schools development and sustainability is thinking broadly about human and financial resources—making best use of all available education and noneducation dollars and combining these financial resources with the human resources of community partners (Finance Project, 2007). In funding community school initiatives, partner organizations should first assess what resources they are able to bring to the planning table and then identify any additional resources they will need, both large and small, to support their efforts. Successful planning teams will quickly discover that the most innovative programs emerge from meetings focused on joint problem solving through partnership.

THE PERSPECTIVES OF A TEACHER EDUCATOR: PROBLEM SOLVING THROUGH PARTNERSHIP

One day while attending the Community School Advisory Board meeting at Edison, the principal and the community school coordinator brought a concern to the partners about the need for an after-school reading program for at-risk students. We were fortunate that an after-school program was already in existence, but SER, the community organization that was running it, was having difficulty finding teachers willing to stay until almost 6:00 p.m., a problem not uncommon to agencies providing childcare services and wanting to provide academic support for their participants.

The problem was further compounded by limits in funding from the state, resulting in Edison's after-school program primarily being staffed by paraprofessionals, artists, and local sports and recreation providers from within the community. This situation proved to be the perfect opportunity to consider a solution that was mutually of benefit to both our organizations and one that wouldn't require the financial expense involved with hiring teachers.

What emerged was an innovative solution satisfying both the school's need for providing tutorial support in reading while simultaneously addressing the college's need to offer a literacy practicum where graduate students could work with children individually to complete their course requirements. The successful implementation of this literacy practicum led to our initiating several other college courses held on-site, expanding these offerings to take place during the school day. In retrospect, it was also the first step to moving beyond my role as professor and supervisor of student teachers to that of liaison between Edison and the college.

In Edison's history as a community school, there are many other similar stories that speak to the ingenuity of its partners in funding key initiatives. Perhaps most important has been the ability of partner leadership to emerge and cross the boundaries of their respective organizations and to generously place at the school's disposal a variety of resources.

CORE COMPETENCY #5: SUPPORTING LEADERSHIP THAT CROSSES BOUNDARIES IN THE COMMUNITY SCHOOL

The Coalition for Community Schools (Blank, Berg, and Melaville, 2006) has coined the term *cross-boundary leadership* and emphasized its critical connection to community schools. Their framework for cross-boundary leadership is akin to the central theme of this book, that the development of children and youth takes place as part of a complex but closely interconnected "educational ecosystem." The Coalition conceives that advocacy for community schools entails producing and mobilizing leaders at various levels, both within and beyond the school setting. They define leadership on three levels: "community leadership," "leadership on the ground," and "leadership in the middle."

As part of the Coalition's framework, local government, civic, corporate, and agency leaders who share a vision and policy commitment to community schools are referred to as "community leaders." Those at the school site who are familiar with local issues are referred to as "leaders on the ground" because they have the skills to build relationships, connect resources, and create opportunities. Their reference to "leaders in the middle" is best represented by organizational managers who are able to connect the idea of community schools within their organizations, who can serve to keep the community school initiative focused by building an infrastructure across organizations, and who can foster alliances among partners.

At the Thomas Edison Elementary School, a multileveled leadership structure similar to that described by the Coalition evolved over time reflecting both formal and informal leadership roles. The community school coordinator best exemplified "on the ground leadership" by effectively managing the school's many partnerships and successfully representing the voice of Edison and the surrounding neighborhood at key community venues, including meetings of the Port Chester Cares Community Coalition. This group successfully engaged local stakeholders, youth representatives, and leaders from various organizations in lending their resources, commitment, and expertise to positive youth development and community advancement.

Parents and teachers at Edison also emerged in what the Coalition would refer to as "leaders on the ground," serving in a variety of capacities as part of the school's leadership infrastructure, which included a number of active committees with broad-based community representation.

Edison's five strategic partners can be conceptualized as having served as "leaders in the middle" given the alliances they forged with each other through integrated programming at the school site and through the use of their political networks and regular contacts with broader social and cultural institutions (for example, communications media and charitable foundations) to promote advocacy and support for this approach to schooling.

Edison's community school allies also included school district personnel, Board of Education members, and government officials, thus representing the Coalition's view of "community leaders" by fulfilling their roles of endorsing policies in favor of community schools and securing funding for continued implementation. This work, in our view, illustrates the viability of Bronfenbrenner's core idea—as we consider the layers of support that were able to come together to surround Edison's children and families through the community schools strategy.

CHAPTER SUMMARY

In this chapter, strategies were provided for initiating a planning process that incorporates a new set of professional skills and knowledge in the design of a community school. This chapter also described how a Strategic Action Plan can be developed based on Human Ecology Theory, resulting in a community school that is better able to respond to the needs of the whole child. In doing so, practical and creative suggestions were provided for finding ways to learn more about children's lives outside of school, about the needs of their families, and about variables beyond the classroom that impact upon student learning.

Components of the Strategic Action Plan were also delineated, along with the elements of effective teamwork, both of which were unpacked in ways that advocate for inclusive representation among a diverse set of partners. The strategies as outlined in this chapter are important because they provide mechanisms for running effective team meetings, resolving conflict in a productive manner, and facilitating interorganizational collaboration, all of which are critical to conducting the business of community schools.

Finally, included in the chapter were suggestions for how best to approach the significant task of funding community school initiatives in ways that truly require thinking "outside the box" and conclude with a discussion about the importance of multileveled leadership in an approach to schooling that attempts to address the needs of students who function at the center of a complex "educational ecosystem." In chapter 3 we turn our attention to teaching, learning, and professional development in the unique setting of the community school.

Chapter Three

Teaching, Learning, and Professional Development in the Community School

The movement to establish community schools both nationally and internationally has grown tremendously over the past decade, and many of these schools have focused their efforts on providing a variety of much-needed health and human services for students and their families. This book further advocates for the implementation of community schools that intentionally integrate instructional practices that promote "community building" at the classroom level, support a positive school climate, and provide a vehicle for sharing the resources of community partners within the classroom to support teaching, learning, and professional development.

Careful forethought about what classrooms should "look and feel like" in the community school should be an integral part of implementation, and planning for teaching, learning, and professional development in this setting can be both invigorating and transformative for a school staff. The Thomas Edison Elementary School explored every dimension of "community building" in its own implementation efforts, and the belief in the importance of connecting the community school to the classroom and to the growth and professional development of teachers continued to guide its work over the years.

Recent research on child development (Shonkoff and Phillips, 2000) has indicated that academic engagement is made possible through the positive and supportive relationships students have with others who play significant roles in the environments in which they learn and grow. In advocating for the expansion of community oriented schools, the director of the Coalition for Community Schools (Coalition for Community Schools, 2009) draws upon this research to remind educators that "engagement precedes achievement" and that community schools serve as the perfect conduit for facilitating such types of relational engagement as they seek to improve the quality of children's lives at home, in school, and in the neighborhood.

At the Thomas Edison Elementary School, "community building" started with implementing strategies that promoted caring relationships among the children and between them and the school's faculty so that both groups could be guided by a schoolwide ethos to care for and serve others. It goes without saying that supporting the professional development of school faculty was required to ensure their commitment to implementing these carefully designed and well-coordinated "community building" initiatives.

Although subsequent chapters will further extend the discussion of "community building" to family engagement and to issues related to their empowerment within the community, the present chapter outlines ways for implementing an approach to community schooling that extends its reach to the classroom.

INSTRUCTIONAL PRACTICES THAT BUILD COMMUNITY AND SUPPORT WHOLE CHILD EDUCATION

Given the premise that "relational engagement" is a prerequisite to successful academic engagement, there is a need for school faculty and staff to establish environments for learning that youngsters feel deeply connected to and respected within, despite their learning challenges or personal backgrounds. In their work on creating caring and engaging classrooms, Nelson, Lott, and Glenn (2000) strengthen the argument for the importance of relational engagement by recommending classroom practices that build upon students' self-esteem, foster self-discipline, and realize their potential by meaningfully and positively connecting them with those who are so much a part of these learning environments.

Similar ideas were reflected in the methods and materials of the Child Development Project (Developmental Studies Center, 1995a, 1995b, 1997, 2004), an approach that had been used at Edison from 1996 through 2006 and that eventually led to the school's successful implementation of character education and to receiving recognition as a National School of Character in 2003 by the Character Education Partnership (CEP), a well-known and respected nonprofit organization committed to the implementation of quality character education programs across the country.

As a scientifically validated model for both violence prevention (U.S. Department of Education, n.d.) and effective character education (Berkowitz and Bier, 2005), the Child Development Project served to introduce the school to their conceptual framework of the new "ABCs" of learning. This framework, with a variety of recommended instructional practices, included as its goal helping students gain "autonomy," experience a sense of "belonging," and to achieve "social, emotional, and intellectual competency" (Developmental Studies Center, 1995a).

Instructional practices of the Child Development Project, in conjunction with others learned and implemented by Edison faculty over the years, provided opportunities for promoting the intellectual growth of children in ways that had been traditionally considered nonacademic and therefore, of little value in the classroom. Once Edison teachers had been given a new lens for understanding children's overall developmental growth, the strategies described below were embraced by them and easily infused across the curriculum, having a major impact on student achievement.

When considering the importance of instructional practices that support "community building efforts" in classrooms, Noddings's (2008) commentary in support of Whole Child Education has direct relevance. In her discussion, she indicated that educators are committing a disservice to both students and society to think that nonacademic activities have no intellectual worth. At Edison, this argument was found to have great merit, and activities with a focus on relationship building were extremely helpful in ensuring student success in both academic and social contexts. Described below are the major community-building strategies used in classrooms and throughout the Thomas Edison Elementary School.

Class Meetings

Class meetings have become increasingly popular and form the mainstay of many character education programs (for example, The Child Development Project and Responsive Classroom). These meetings typically involve gathering the entire class together in an area designated for this purpose for approximately thirty minutes in order to participate in class discussions around a variety of topics and student concerns.

Class meetings are an important part of building a classroom community and have been used successfully for teaching both academic and interpersonal skills. As part of these meetings, Edison students resolved problems as part of the class, participated in planning classroom activities, and learned how to reflect as well as self-assess their efforts in school. Safe and supportive classroom environments were thus established for sharing feelings, perspectives, and experiences, with the added benefit of these meetings helping to promote children's academic growth in the areas of critical thinking, language development, and problem solving.

Cross-age Learning Opportunities: "Buddy" Class Partnerships

The Child Development Project recommends the pairing of older and younger students as part of a "buddy class" relationship used to promote caring, learning, and language development across the grades (Developmental Studies

Center, 1997). At Edison, this buddy class relationship entailed meeting about once or twice a month for younger and older student pairs to complete an activity that might involve sharing a story or completing a project together.

Cross-age Learning Opportunities: Intergrade Meetings

Cross-age learning opportunities were expanded at Edison to include intergrade meetings held several times yearly. Intergrade meetings involved total school participation in small discussion groups led by a school staff member or by members of partner organizations familiar to the children. Held schoolwide, at the same time and in relation to the same topic, these meetings were focused on social skills development, solving school problems, and setting individual or group goals. Intergrade meetings, as in the sample activity presented, were created by the school's Character Education Committee and proved to be extremely useful in developing important skills for communication.

Schoolwide Unity Builders

Conceptualized by the Child Development Project (Developmental Studies Center, 1995a), schoolwide unity builders are activities designed to enhance the spirit of community within the school while minimizing student disadvantage. Such disadvantages become most apparent during events fostering the kind of competition that unintentionally place individuals at the center of unfavorable attention or reflect the educational and financial disparities between families in a school.

Edison teachers reshaped many of its schoolwide activities to encourage family involvement that was both fun and engaging but not dependent upon extrinsic rewards or unfair forms of competition. They instituted, for example, Family Math Nights and student publishing celebrations, both of which gave parents a wonderful and comfortable venue for them to interact with their children around school curriculum and to receive hands-on knowledge about how to support their children's learning.

One schoolwide unity builder that proved to be highly successful in turning around the once negative image that Edison had within the community, as a result of its high levels of poverty and immigrant student population, was its annual "Gallery Walk." This evening event featured exhibitions of student work based upon grade level thematic units of study.

Involving total community participation (with attendance exceeding several hundred guests), the Gallery Walk transformed Edison into a colorful, exciting, and print-rich museum gallery with students at each grade level serving as docents, proudly sharing the knowledge they had gained through

Textbox 3.1. Sample Intergrade Meeting

**The Boy with the Blue Hair: It's OK to Walk
Away from Put-Downs**
Goals of the first intergrade meeting:

- To encourage children to be tolerant of one another
- To encourage children to practice kindness and sensitivity toward others
- To enable children to think about the short- and long-term consequences of put-downs
- To enable children to accept who and what they are and appreciate their own strengths and uniqueness
- To provide children with strategies for dealing with put-downs

Materials:

- Boy with the Blue Hair Poster for each facilitator to be printed by technology assistant
- Easel stand, chart paper, marker, blue tape

Task:
Conversation Starter: Teachers or other facilitators begin by noting that everyone, at some point, has said something mean to someone (to put someone down) or has experienced being put down by another person. Ask the children to share such examples, based upon their experiences, and to describe their feelings when it happened (for example, anger, hurt, and embarrassment). The feelings they articulate are recorded. Be sure the children understand that there is no right or wrong answer at this time.

Scenario Introduction: The Boy with the Blue Hair
Teachers tell the students that today's discussion will be about "put-downs" and how to handle them by thinking through the choices, especially when adults are not around.

Teachers introduce the following scenario: Everyone noticed that the new student in school had blue hair unlike anyone else's (although there are certainly many other children in the world with blue hair). The boy was born with blue hair, and he didn't really like it but knew that he was born that way and there wasn't really much he could do about it as hair dye hadn't been invented yet. In class, a few of his classmates called him "blue head." Feeling hurt and angry, the boy with the blue hair told the teacher, and the name-calling stopped "temporarily" after his teacher had a class meeting.

Stop and Think Discussion Point 1:
Tolerance, Kindness, and Self-Acceptance
Teachers ask the children to briefly mention something about themselves that they might not like and wish they could change.

Children are then asked, "How might you feel if you were born with blue hair and your peers were putting you down?"

Teachers use this "Stop and Think" point of discussion to discuss tolerance, kindness, and self-acceptance.

Stop and Think Discussion Point 2: Responding to Put-Downs
Teachers continue the scenario about the boy with the blue hair by describing how, on the way home from school, several classmates started calling him "blue head" again. The teacher asks the question, "What choices does the boy with the blue hair have now in dealing with the situation?"

Teachers emphasize thinking ahead about the consequences of their actions and note that the boy with the blue hair decided to challenge one of the name-callers to a fight.

Teachers ask the question, "What will be the consequences of his choice to make this kind of a challenge?" Teachers should acknowledge that the teasing might stop with the boy punching the other child in the nose, but the long-term negative consequences of having to fight all of your life as a way of handling put-downs should be emphasized.

Teachers elicit what better choices the boy with the blue hair might have (particularly since no adults were around when the incident happened) in dealing with the situation immediately and in the long term, and their answers should be recorded. Their responses should include ignoring these remarks, being honest about one's feelings, taking a deep breath and walking away, sharing feelings, and getting the support of an adult ally.

Stop and Think Discussion Point 3: Wrap Up
Teachers wrap up the discussion by asking students to summarize what they have learned about "put-downs" from the intergrade meeting. Possible discussion points include:

- Live out our school's core values of respect, responsibility, kindness, and tolerance
- Think about the long- and short-term consequences of all that you say and do
- Accept yourself and appreciate your own uniqueness
- It's OK to walk away from a put-down
- It's important to share your feelings with an adult who can help
- Recognize that using the Internet to send verbal messages is another form of verbal put-down with negative consequences
- Remind each other of the "boy with the blue hair story" when what someone says makes you uncomfortable at Edison

Helpful hint: In addressing incidents of put-downs in the class, teachers should make reference to the intergrade meeting and the boy with the blue hair.

their learning projects. This event experience would play a critical role in enabling the community at large to understand that access to quality education is possible even in the poorest neighborhoods.

Town Meetings

Representing another type of schoolwide community building activity, town meetings involved assembling students within or across grade levels for a specific purpose. At Edison, these meetings were held for the following reasons: to establish schoolwide student expectations, to provide recognition for their efforts and achievements, to pay homage to individuals past and present who had made a contribution to the school, to give students another forum to engage in public speaking on schoolwide matters, and to conduct year-end reflections. The school year was brought to closure each June, for example, with a town meeting for all students highlighting the year's events and bidding them a fond farewell for the summer.

Home-School Connections

An important goal for all community schools is increasing family involvement, and many districts implementing this approach to school reform collect extensive data to gauge parent participation at all schoolwide events, programs, and activities. The idea, however, of engaging parents as "part" of the classroom curriculum is a unique feature of the Child Development Project, and Edison began to extend its reach to families in this endeavor early on as part of its journey in becoming a community school.

In implementing the parent component of the Child Development Project, students took home meaningful activities on a regular basis that were designed to encourage "family discussions" about aspects of their cultural heritage and family traditions that were then shared in the classroom and integrated into the curriculum. The value of these bilingual take-home activities was that they instilled in students a sense of pride in their diverse family backgrounds and engaged parents in classwork in ways that transcended the need for high levels of formal education. Equally as important, teachers gained a deeper knowledge about students' lives outside of school, thereby enabling each and every child to feel genuinely connected to their classroom.

Developmental Discipline

Developmental discipline has been incorporated into many Character Education Programs, including, for example, both the Child Development Project and the Responsive Classroom. This approach helps strengthen relational engagement between adults and children, while also helping students become more autonomous and intrinsically motivated. Developmental discipline emphasizes nonpunitive approaches to addressing misbehavior by engaging students in the process of "constructing" classroom rules or group norms for their behavior and by encouraging proactive classroom management strategies.

A developmental approach to discipline considers not only the age of the child in deciding how any disciplinary infraction should be handled but also, and perhaps most importantly, takes into consideration the social-emotional state of the individual. A scenario in which a boy comes to school wearing a cap that violates the "no hat in school" rule best illustrates this approach. Rather than forcing the student to remove his cap, the teacher who is developmental in approaching discipline investigates further and, in discovering that the child is mortified about his new hair cut, will allow the child to keep his cap on for several days, maintain his dignity, and use the class meeting format to discuss why rules need to be flexible at times.

Other examples of developmentally appropriate strategies used at Edison to address disciplinary issues while simultaneously attempting to develop students' social-emotional, ethical, and intellectual competencies have involved the following:

1. Helping students think through alternative behaviors using the class meeting format.
2. Encouraging those involved in a disagreement to use conflict-resolution skills with the goal of reaching a compromise in which there are no losers.
3. Developing a plan for restitution or "making things right again."
4. Teaching both children and parents to use a common language for addressing discipline based upon the school's core values.
5. Establishing a strong character education program that enables teachers to see themselves as responsible for teaching and modeling the traits of "good character" they would like to see in their students.

Edison's Core Values

At Edison, core values referred to the explicitly taught universal traits of good character, which served to frame the relationships and interactions of all members of the school community. These core values, developed with the children and other key stakeholders, were integrated into all of the community-building strategies that have been described, and they included the character traits of "respect," "responsibility," "kindness," and "tolerance."

Service Learning

Service learning opportunities are an important way in which to connect students to a community beyond the classroom and to concerns and needs other than their own. Through participation in meaningful service projects—locally, nationally, or worldwide—students are able to bring to life the school's core values and actively engage in the kind of problem solving that requires critical thinking, ingenuity, and the integration of academic content.

Students and teachers at Edison participated in a variety of service projects each year within different school contexts. Service projects were included as grade-level activities, as part of special club offerings held after school, and on a schoolwide basis. One of Edison's most distinctive accomplishments as a community school, from which the surrounding neighborhood benefitted, was to work with Habitat for Humanity, local officials, and students from the district's high school to build a house in Port Chester for a qualifying family whose prospects for homeownership would otherwise have been minimal.

The preceding section of this chapter described how the basic tenets of a community school can be easily integrated throughout the instructional day and help schools meet the critical challenge of individualizing and differentiating their practices. The community school espoused by the authors of this book is one in which strong academic teaching is supported by the cross-curricular integration of the various "community building" strategies that have been described. However, this book also advocates for the critical role of community school partners in lending their expertise to the classroom by providing behavioral and academic interventions beyond what can be delivered by the regular classroom teacher and by offering consultative support to school staff.

RESPONSE TO INTERVENTION AND COMMUNITY SCHOOLS

An important federal initiative, referred to as Response to Intervention or "RTI," unfolded in 2007 to ensure success for all students. With the immediate goals of improving learning and behavioral outcomes for those identified as being at risk of school failure, RTI mandates a multileveled schoolwide intervention system in which decision making is continuously informed by data (National Center on Response to Intervention, 2010). Undoubtedly, RTI will pave the way for furthering the opportunities for interorganizational collaboration in ways that will directly benefit these youngsters.

The multileveled structures of RTI translate into a host of services that involve screening for the early identification of those falling below grade-level performance benchmarks, monitoring their progress over time, implementing research-based instructional practices with these students, and offering graduated or intensifying levels of instructional support for those not responding to services already in place. Although RTI interventions require more close collaboration than ever before between classroom teachers and support staff, the primary responsibility for their delivery still rests almost entirely with school personnel, who are considered "interventionists" under this framework.

The connections may not yet be evident to many educators and policymakers, but our work has led us to conclude that the intent of RTI to be comprehensive and results oriented parallels the intent of community schools across the country. However, while initiatives undertaken under RTI are designed to address the academic or behavioral concerns of students as they manifest themselves in classrooms, they may fail to address the root causes of their difficulties. These difficulties may stem from or be further exacerbated by the need for adequate nutrition, health care, and housing, together with the need to be free from the psychological and emotional stresses of growing up in poverty.

We champion the idea that community schools can play an important role in significantly enhancing a school's capacity to meet and even go beyond

RTI requirements. Their potential to be successful in this endeavor results from the fact that partner organizations are able to buttress the efforts of school personnel by mobilizing their own resources or those of other community organizations to help remove any barriers that are likely to impede student learning.

At the Thomas Edison Elementary School, partners enhanced RTI initiatives through a "one stop, engage all" approach to supporting the whole child. For example, as part of initial RTI interventions, designed to support academically at-risk students whose class placement was within the general education setting, Manhattanville College was able implement a number of valuable programs and services. The first secured individual tutoring for many of these youngsters through site-based courses held during the school day and after school, as part of its PDS offerings.

In addition, the college was successful at obtaining funding from the Reading Reform Foundation to provide special literacy training, before the start of the school year, for two classroom teachers and one special education collaborative/RTI teacher. These teachers all had groups of students who were not responding to the teaching of reading, writing, and spelling as part of the general education curriculum in the first grade. The foundation also provided accompanying instructional materials for this initiative with in-class modeling, coaching, and coplanning assistance from an accredited staff developer.

Coaching activities with the three teachers participating in the program ensured that the protocols of the multisensory teaching strategy used were delivered with integrity. In addition, several members of the college faculty decided to undertake the project as a form of practitioner inquiry research so that both the school and the college could benefit from its research contributions in the field of literacy development.

Data collected during the first year of implementation of the Reading Reform initiative appeared promising, with 66 percent of participating first graders meeting grade-level expectations on the Gates-MacGinitie Reading Test of Vocabulary administered toward the end of the school year and 32 percent performing a year or more above grade level on this assessment. Furthermore, 91 percent of the same cohort of first graders, given the Morrison-McCall Word Test in late spring, met grade-level expectations on this assessment, with 43 percent of these students performing at least a year or more above grade level on this test.

As a final point, in comparing the cohort of first graders involved with Reading Reform to the previous year's cohort who were not taught this method of reading, 78 percent of the Reading Reform students exited the grade-level scoring at benchmark on the Dynamic Indicators of Basic Early Literacy Skills (DIBELS) assessment used for progress monitoring while only 63 percent of those who had not been exposed to this program reached benchmark the year before. Planning for the following year included expanding this approach to literacy instruction in the second grade.

Supporting more intensive intervention measures under RTI, another of Edison's community partners came forward to provide assistance and secure the expertise of a major medical facility in dealing with the school's most behaviorally challenging students. The program was designed as part of a three-year study by a hospital in New York City and delivered by the social worker from the Guidance Center, Edison's partner in the delivery of mental health services.

Training for the social worker by the hospital's staff included working with the parents and guardians, of the twelve students who had been identified for the program, on effective parenting strategies. The students selected by teachers and support staff were those who had not responded adequately to the implementation of various behavior management plans executed by school personnel within the classroom and in other settings throughout the building. What was particularly noteworthy about this program was its focus on providing discipline strategies for parents and modifying the dynamics of family life as a prerequisite to improving in-school behavior.

The program took place over ten sessions with participating families meeting weekly and receiving weekly follow-up check-ins throughout the year thereafter from the social worker involved. Initial results of the first year of the study indicate that 100 percent of the students whose parents completed the program showed an improvement in student behavior and 80 percent showed improvement in academic performance as measured through teacher surveys and final report cards. Furthermore, surveys of the parents of these students indicated their feeling empowered to implement the strategies they had learned during these sessions.

Similar to RTI, community schools are committed to the success of students by being data driven and comprehensive in their delivery of services. However, community schools have the potential to achieve this and so much more through their emphasis on integrating the resources of the community at the school site, their ability to widen the picture's lens about what students need to be successful, and to extend their reach in support of families and the surrounding neighborhood, recognizing that all play a pivotal role. These schools think more broadly about student outcomes and draw from more extensive research, not solely limited to research on what works in educational practice but from what has been demonstrated as effective from research in the fields of psychology, sociology, health, and human services.

Furthermore, while RTI is mostly perceived as an "on your own strategy" in which school personnel are charged with figuring out among themselves what must be done to ensure student success, community schools embrace the old African adage, "It takes a whole village to raise a child." As experts in our respective fields, we advocate for the community school as a reform strategy that can help facilitate, through partnership and collaboration, the goals and mandates of RTI. These goals and mandates are otherwise likely to be constrained by the traditional school day, divided among an already overextended group of professionals, and may result in a band-aid treatment for the children they are intended to serve.

AUTHENTIC AND JOB-EMBEDDED PROFESSIONAL DEVELOPMENT WITHIN A COMMUNITY SCHOOL

As indicated in the first chapter of this book, the Children's Aid Society has generated, based on their work with community schools across the country, a set of defining characteristics describing community schools as a results-oriented "strategy" focused upon student success, rather than as a singular, prepackaged program. They further describe the community school as a place characterized by extended services, hours, relationships, and partnerships (Children's Aid Society, 2001). By the very nature of this expanded network of relationships, the community school provides the perfect venue for enhancing teacher knowledge and the further development of all professionals engaged in partnership with the school.

Over the years, Edison teachers both deepened and broadened their understanding regarding almost every aspect of child development through the school's collaborative partnerships. They had the opportunity to learn from these partners and community leaders about the family stresses that often impact upon academic achievement, and they achieved a better understanding of such important issues as bullying, its causes and prevention. In addition, they also gained a greater awareness about the prevalence and impact of common childhood illnesses, such as asthma, on classroom learning. Finally, the community school strategy afforded teachers from Edison access to ongoing professional development through its status as a Professional Development School (PDS).

THE PRINCIPAL'S PERSPECTIVE: PROFESSIONAL DEVELOPMENT WITHIN A COMMUNITY SCHOOL

Consistent with the characteristics of community schools so aptly described by the Children's Aid Society, Edison faculty had the unique opportunity to

flexibly use the resources of the school site and those of their partners to pro-
vide customized training and job-embedded professional development during
the school day, after school hours, and in the summer. A wonderful example
of this occurred each year when faculty members would go off to the beautiful
campus of their college partner to conduct a year-end retreat.

The Edison staff retreat represented a nonattendance day for its students
and one in which the school's staff were engaged in a number of critical tasks.
The day's agenda included team building, reviewing student achievement
data, and for the period of time in which a literacy consultant had worked
with the staff (from 2001 to 2007), her participation at the retreat would al-
low her to share some year-end reflections on what had been accomplished
as a result of their work on implementing balanced literacy instruction. Staff
would also have the opportunity, each and every year, to give their input on
what future professional development should take place.

Holding the retreat off site also served to provide focused and uninter-
rupted time for teachers to engage in student articulation discussions. These
discussions would be focused on students' strengths and individual needs
across each of the developmental domains of their growth and learning.
Finally, part of the day would also be devoted to sharing all that had been
accomplished in support of Whole Child Education through partnership.

One of the most memorable retreat formats we ever had included parents
participating in a panel discussion to talk about their own experiences at-
tending schools outside of the United States and to share the expectations
they had for both the school and their children. These discussions, which
included opportunities for dialogue between teachers and parents, were con-
ducted bilingually with the help of our case manager and served to provide
lessons on parental involvement that one simply cannot get from a workshop.

With a well-developed history of collaboration, the experiences of staff
and community school partners at Edison gave life to a motto that has been
shared at conferences and workshops across the country and is represented in
the title of the next section.

"THE PROFESSIONAL DEVELOPMENT SCHOOL + THE COMMUNITY SCHOOL = ONE POWERFUL ALLIANCE"

A professional development school (PDS) is typically defined in terms of
a collaborative relationship between a college and a local school for the
purposes of teacher preparation, the professional development of practicing teachers, research about teaching and learning, and the improvement of

student achievement. In the area of teacher preparation, significant research indicates what we have experienced professionally, that many newly hired teachers find themselves working in isolation with children facing a multitude of challenges impacting upon their school success (Darling-Hammond, 1994, Zeichner, 1996).

Lacking both preservice preparation in Whole Child Education and working in traditional school settings where there is a lack of knowledge and resources for this type of approach, it is not uncommon for new teachers to leave the profession within their initial three to five years. It is also no surprise that a high level of teacher turnover has frequently been associated with schools serving poor children, whose parents often exert little influence in the districts they attend and have limited access to resources and opportunities.

Edison successfully responded to these challenges through its implementation of a PDS relationship that was uniquely situated within a community school. In doing so, this alliance served as fertile ground for the development of many pioneering and inventive school practices. The diagram below illustrates the distinctive features of both the Professional Development School and the community school, also highlighting their overlapping characteristics.

If a school is to be successful at incorporating both of these approaches into a working organizational entity, both the distinctive and common characteristics of each must be considered in the planning process. However, this process requires a delicate balance between providing clarity and specificity about how each partnership will be implemented at the outset through formal agreements, while allowing for other aspects of these partnerships to grow organically.

When situating or embedding a PDS partnership within a community school, formal agreements or Memoranda of Understanding (sometimes referred to as an MOU) are particularly useful in addressing the often-problematic use of space, time, personnel, and resources. For example, as a result of Edison being used to full capacity, it was specified early on in the MOU that Manhattanville College would be allocated a shared space with the Guidance Center's caseworker to conduct its meetings, courses, and related activities.

The colocation of both community school partners within the same physical space would serve as a catalyst for interorganizational collaboration. This type of collaboration is a feature common to community schools but not necessarily widespread in most PDS schools. Collaboration between these "roommates" thus began with a discussion around scheduling the use of a shared space but then organically grew into an idea that would eventually involve student teachers planning and conducting, with the caseworker, a variety of parent workshops around such relevant topics as Internet safety and homework help.

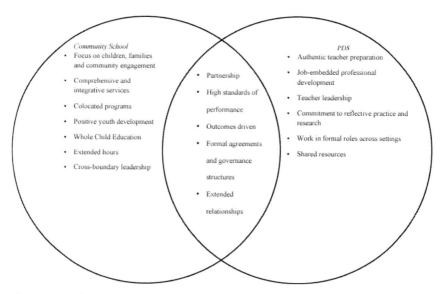

Figure 3.1. The PDS and the Community School

It is important to underscore the feature of "high performance standards" included in figure 3.1, common to both the community school and PDS, because of the critical role they played at Edison over the years in improving student outcomes and, equally as important, in advancing the professional practices of all involved.

Given the network of partners operating within a community school, maintaining "high performance standards" for employees of these organizations requires that they not only meet the quality assurance indicators of their respective organizations but that they also extend their reach to support the mission of the school and the work of other partners. Clearly, successfully incorporating the community school and PDS into one powerful alliance requires marrying the distinctive and common features of both these initiatives.

A community school/PDS partnership is best developed incrementally with specific components grown from the needs of all participants. At the Thomas Edison Elementary School, its alliance with Manhattanville College was established with the goal of advancing student learning, professional development, and teacher education. Each of the PDS initiatives undertaken in support of this goal over the course of a decade is illustrated in table 3.1. They represent the ideas of the Professional Development School Committee, one of several important working groups that functioned as part of Edison's community school leadership infrastructure.

The community school/PDS alliance that had been formed proved to be beneficial to all of Edison's partners, giving them opportunities to gain first-

Table 3.1. Components of the Thomas Edison Community School/Manhattanville College PDS Partnership

Components	Participants	Activities	Evidence-Based Outcomes: (i.e., determined via data analysis of surveys, observations, interviews, and student assessments)
Student Teaching	Student teachers, cooperating teachers, PDS liaison	Student Teaching: Student teaching experiences enhanced by weekly seminars held at the school site by the PDS liaison and by their required participation at faculty meetings and community school events	Outcomes for students: Individual attention and instruction, more schoolwork accomplished, greater opportunities for special projects, and improved student achievement. Outcomes for teachers: Increased teacher leadership and refinement of instructional practices
	Partner organizations, community school coordinator	Community School Partner Shadowing: Student teachers follow partner providers and reflect upon the work of these professionals in support of Whole Child Education	Outcomes for student teachers: Greater understanding of Whole Child Education and cross-boundary leadership in working with a myriad of professionals, understanding the value of engaging
	Family case manager	Family and Community Engagement: Student teachers plan for parent education workshops with case manager	families, and learning the value of "making contributions through service projects" that support classroom instruction and the school community
	Cooperating teachers and PDS liaison	Legacy Projects: Extends service learning opportunities to student teachers responsible for identifying a need and creating a project with a long-lasting impact to the school community	For school administration: Facilitated recruitment of new teacher hires

Table 3.1. Components of the Thomas Edison Community School/Manhattanville College PDS Partnership

Components	Participants	Activities	Evidence-Based Outcomes: (i.e., determined via data analysis of surveys, observations, interviews, and student assessments)
On-site College Courses	College professors and/or qualified school faculty serving as adjuncts or guest presenters	College Courses: Courses for school faculty held at the school or at the college	Outcomes for teachers of course offerings: Needs- and interest-based staff development focused on continuous growth (at no cost or at a reduced rate); more teachers qualify for salary increments based on ongoing coursework and job-embedded professional development
	College professors and classroom teachers	Methods Courses: Courses for preservice teachers, who are involved in structured classroom observations and tutoring during or after school	Outcomes for preservice teachers: Authentic teacher preparation experiences involving culturally and linguistically diverse students
	Preservice teachers and PDS liaison	Triad Teaching: College professor, classroom teacher, and preservice teachers coteach to enrich curriculum content	
New Teacher Induction	PDS liaison, mentor teachers, and first- and second-year teachers	PDS liaison trains master teachers from the school to serve as mentors to first- and second-year teachers and facilitates monthly meetings with mentors and new teachers at the school site	Outcomes for teachers: Promoted teacher leadership, collegiality, and commitment to Whole Child Education Outcomes for school administration: Helped to ensure new teacher success and retention

Summer Programming	College and school faculty members, preservice teachers, school-based health center staff, and participating students	Preservice teachers serve as teachers in the summer program with experienced teachers from the school serving as their instructional coaches. College and school faculty coordinate activities with health services provided by the school-based health center.	Outcomes for students: Greater retention of academic content over the summer months Outcomes for teachers: Promoted teacher leadership Outcomes for preservice teachers: Authentic preservice teaching experiences Outcomes for families: Instructional support and childcare provided during summer months
College Partner Campus Visitation	Teachers of grade five students entering the middle school, their students and parents Student teachers and preservice volunteers from the college College faculty and its administrative staff volunteers	Visit to the campus of college includes admission information, orientation to college life, campus tour, hands-on demonstrations, and visits to college classroom	Outcomes for students and parents: Exposure to college as a viable option in planning their futures

hand knowledge about the challenges of teaching, to become grounded in the philosophy and practices of Whole Child Education, and to extend the work of their organizations to the planning and implementation of meaningful pre-service training and professional development.

Partnerships between colleges and universities, with the responsibility of educating our next generation of teachers, and community schools are ideal for establishing the PDS partnership activities described in table 3.1. We have found this type of partnership to be critical to ensuring that teaching, at all levels of experience, remains "responsive, collaborative, and transformative."

In our view, teaching that is "responsive" reflects those practices that have been described earlier in this chapter as they actively incorporate relational engagement and community building, address the broad developmental needs of children and youth, and promote growth in both academic and social contexts. The implication is that such practices must also be "transformative," reflecting teachers' abilities to adapt and change based upon the individual needs of their students from year to year, and "collaborative" in that they require the support of all others involved in school partnership.

As a vibrant and dynamic learning community, Edison was easily able to recruit the best teacher candidates from Manhattanville College to join its faculty from a pool already familiar with the school's mission and culture. Coming full circle in their own careers, these professionals would achieve tenure and later serve as collaborating teachers for new groups of preservice teachers. As one former student teacher, who is now tenured and hosting others preparing to enter the profession, once noted, "Working in a professional development school has given me an academic resource—a laboratory for study, learning and growth." It is thus easy to understand how Edison's community school/PDS partnership helped overcome the difficulties of recruitment, induction, and retention endemic to many schools with high levels of poverty.

CHAPTER SUMMARY

Recognizing that effective "academic engagement is preceded by strong relational engagement," several strategies for "community building" were introduced in this chapter. These strategies, for implementation at both the classroom and school levels, were intentionally designed to help realize the goal of establishing relational engagement in all school settings, with the added benefits of transforming instructional practice, creating a more positive school climate, improving home-school connections, and ultimately increasing student achievement.

Chapter 3 also articulated the ways in which community schools are uniquely positioned, via their design and delivery of services through partnership and their commitment to educating the whole child, to facilitate teaching that is responsive to individual needs, transformative rather than static, and collaborative rather than isolated. In doing so, we stress the importance of building a school-university partnership in which professional development and teacher commitment are held in high esteem and provide readers with suggestions for forming this relationship.

Lastly, we advocate for using community schools as a vehicle for realizing federal or local policy mandates that require intervening on behalf of our most at-risk students by applying a "one stop, engage all" approach to removing barriers to learning, providing easy access to community resources at the school site, and engaging partners in the efforts of school personnel to help children succeed.

Chapter Four

Community Schools as a Results-Oriented Strategy

Recognizing the intense national focus on using student achievement data at all levels of decision making, this chapter begins with revisiting the Strategic Action Plan as a document aimed at achieving results. The plan's inclusion of evaluation strategies that specify the student performance data and community school outcomes to be examined contributes to the document's ability to support continuous improvement at all stages of maturation within the community school's development.

The present chapter also introduces the idea of external validation as yet another important method of evaluation, using documentation provided by educational researchers affiliated with colleges and universities, external consultants, interested nonprofit organizations, and even state education officials. Several of these entities provided external validation of the work that had taken place at the Thomas Edison Elementary School, documenting its contributions to professional knowledge in the fields of community schools, collaborative leadership, effective instructional practices, and teacher education.

As community school practitioners, we recommend varied methods of evaluation, including the collection of data that will not only show levels of academic performance and progress but will also convey important information about the lives of students and their families not generally included in a "data warehouse" about student achievement. We advocate for evaluation strategies that reveal important information on such factors as student attendance, health and wellness, disciplinary referrals and suspensions, family engagement, and teacher growth and development because all of these factors serve to either facilitate or impede student learning.

In addition to citing examples of how evaluation had been conducted at the Thomas Edison Elementary School, this chapter will also share how the evaluation process has unfolded in community schools across the country.

Thus, readers will be encouraged to think both broadly and deeply about community school outcomes and about ways they can be deliberate about the collection and interpretation of meaningful data.

Finally, this chapter revisits the notion of reciprocal benefits introduced in the first chapter to illustrate how partner organizations are better able to realize their organizational missions in the community school setting and how districts and the surrounding community benefit from their association with these schools as well. The chapter thus enables school practitioners to apply and adapt to their own setting what has already been learned about community schools as a results-oriented strategy.

EVALUATING RESULTS FOR CONTINUOUS IMPROVEMENT IN THE STRATEGIC ACTION PLAN

Five core competencies for designing and implementing a community school were identified earlier as part of chapter 2, with Core Competency #2 centered on the development of the Strategic Action Plan as a tool for evaluation and continuous improvement. At Edison, developing a three-year Strategic Action Plan represented a reasonable amount of time to implement and assess the effectiveness of their initiatives as a community school. However, it was also the school's practice to monitor progress yearly in order to inform decision making and make adjustments along the way.

Chapter 2 presented excerpts from two such plans in tables 2.2 and 2.3, plotting a course of action that took place between 1996 and 1999 aimed at improving student performance in English Language Arts (ELA) and increasing family and community engagement. The objectives included are statements of measurable outcomes related to each of the plan's goals. For example, as part of the 1996 to 1997 Strategic Action Plan, Edison established the goal of improving student achievement in ELA while also introducing teachers to the new learning standards that would later prevail as part of a national movement. This national movement would eventually lead to major changes in the content and format of state assessments.

In determining the efficacy of actions steps taken to improve ELA performance as outlined in the 1996 to 1997 Strategic Action Plan, a related objective required an annual "satisfactory" performance rating for at least 90 percent of teachers in the initial implementation of standards-based instruction within their classrooms. This rating would be based upon an examination of teacher planbooks, student work samples, classroom displays, and both formal and informal classroom observations.

An additional objective pertaining to student performance in ELA provided both annual benchmarks and summative performance expectations for the end of a three-year period by indicating that the third grade, the only grade tested at the time, would demonstrate a 10 percent annual growth measure in the total number of students scoring at or above the State Reference Point (SRP) for each year of the plan's implementation until a 90 percent pass rate had been achieved on these state tests of reading comprehension.

Strategic planning meetings held during the summer examined the school's growth toward achieving its stated objectives. Data related to the literacy goal proposed in the 1996 to 1997 Strategic Action Plan, and its first objective describing the performance expectations for classroom teachers, indicated that all had met the criterion established by demonstrating satisfactory growth in applying the district training they had received in standards-based instruction.

In relation to the second literacy objective contained in the plan, the data indicated that this objective had been exceeded. Where once 83 percent had reached the required State Reference Point during the 1995 to 1996 school year, just prior to Edison becoming a community school, 97 percent achieved SRP in 1996 to 1997 and 95 percent met this performance level in 1997 to 1998, with both of these testing cycles occurring during Edison's adoption of the community school strategy. It is important to point out that the comparison of third grade performance scores for the years cited involved the same test format with the measurement of reading comprehension by the state based on the correct identification of missing words in cloze passages.

CONTRIBUTORS TO EARLY SUCCESS

Summer planning meetings held in 1998 resulted in reframing some of the literacy activities proposed in the 1996 to 1997 Strategic Action Plan to include a more intense focus on implementing the New York State English Language Arts frameworks. The plan proposed developing a common language for literacy instruction across the grades and putting into place specific instructional practices that included increasing student autonomy across the content areas and using informal assessments to guide instruction in all grades. These action steps would find their way into future plans as they proved to be highly successful in improving student achievement and increased Edison's focus on moving children beyond merely passing the test to achieving at high levels of proficiency.

The evaluation strategies contained in the school's next Strategic Action Plan, developed in 1998 to 1999, responded to major changes in the state testing program. It included an ELA performance objective stating that the number of students passing the redesigned state assessment in this area, administered to the fourth grade for the first time, would increase from 19 percent during the first year of the plan's implementation to 39 percent the following year. To achieve the plan's summative performance expectation, at least an 80 percent pass rate was proposed for the end of the third year. The percentage of students actually passing the ELA assessment during the second and third year of the plan's implementation were 61 percent and 84 percent respectively, thereby surpassing the criteria established for this objective.

THE PRINCIPAL'S PERSPECTIVE: THE VALUE OF SUMMER STRATEGIC PLANNING

The process of evaluating results for continuous improvement is best exemplified by Edison's summer strategic planning process. This process took place at a minimal cost when compared to other district expenditures and proved to be well worth the expense. As a follow-up to Edison's year-end staff retreat, teachers representing each grade level, along with support staff, myself as principal, and the community school coordinator, would flesh out the details of the school's Strategic Action Plan. However, we also spent valuable time identifying students for Title I remediation, RTI interventions, and other services available through our partners.

We quickly realized that the ensuing discussions were as important as coming up with a written plan to improve levels of student achievement. These meetings led to meaningful discussions about pedagogy and, in moving our collective thinking to a deeper level, about what it means to be a teacher in a community school. My personal recollections of summer planning sessions are that they would help to develop teacher leadership and make it possible for Edison to respond to changes in school testing and accountability in the years ahead. Since then, I have held firmly to the belief that leadership requires being able to see both the forest and the trees and to always be prepared for the change in seasons.

RESPONDING TO CHANGING CONTEXTS IN ACCOUNTABILITY: AN ECOLOGICAL PERSPECTIVE

Significant changes took place in assessing student achievement from 1999 to 2011, reflecting dramatic shifts in the nation's political, economic, and ideological landscape. Table 4.1 provides an overview of student achievement at the Thomas Edison Elementary School from 1996 to 2011 and integrates into this analysis the Ecological Systems perspective that has informed our work about community schools and remained central to our commitment of using theory to inform practice.

We have placed Ravitch's (2010) historical review of the recent waves of school reform in public education as the backdrop for our analysis of student achievement, raising the likelihood of similar patterns emerging in other schools across the country. The first of these changes took place in 1998 to 1999 when the New York State (NYS) testing program was moved from third to fourth grade with a complete overhaul of the format, content, and scoring of assessments in reading and mathematics to reflect the newly adopted State Learning Standards.

Table 4.1 identifies the most prominent political trends during the period from 1996 to 2001 beginning with former President Clinton's Goals 2000 initiative serving as the catalyst for the development of the New York State Learning Standards and the redesign of state assessments. We place these trends, along with their ideological sentiments, at the Exosystem and Macrosystem levels of our conceptual framework, as these interconnected systems (in which students do not directly participate) have a tremendous impact upon individual students, the schools they attend, the dynamics of their classrooms, and family life.

The new state assessments in English Language Arts (ELA) would eliminate the cloze passages that had once been used to determine a student's reading level, based on a state-established reference point (SRP). Instead, the student's level of "proficiency" in ELA would be determined in relation to reading comprehension, and listening and writing as well. Parallel changes in the New York State mathematics assessments were also implemented to align test content with new standards that emphasized mathematical reasoning and problem solving. For the first time, in addition to multiple-choice responses in the test format, students would be required to show in writing the thought processes they had used to obtain their answers.

The 2002 federal No Child Left Behind (NCLB) legislation and the revision of the Individuals with Disabilities Act (IDEA) in 2004 would place an evolving spotlight on ways to close the achievement gap and on developing systems for holding schools and districts accountable for the performance of minority and special education students so that they would have better access to a high-quality education and be prepared for college. These influences, positioned at the Exosystem and Macrosystem levels in Table 4.1, set into motion specific mandates from 2001 to 2008 governing the participation of special education students and English Language Learners in state testing programs throughout the country.

New York State assessments were expanded to include grades three through five in 2005 to 2006, and in subsequent years nearly all students in

Table 4.1. Ecological Systems Theory Applied to a Historical Analysis of Student Achievement, Showing the Percentage of Edison Students Passing New York State Assessments in English Language Arts and Mathematics from 1996 to 2011

1996–2000 Exosystem and Macrosystem Variables	2001–2008 Exosystem and Macrosystem Variables	2009–2011 Exosystem and Macrosystem Variables
The National Backdrop Behind Student Achievement: President Clinton's "Goals 2000" calls for improved performance in reading and mathematics with federal funding allocated for the development of state standards and assessments ushering in the Learning Standards Movement. Congress charges National Institute of Child Health and Human Development (NICHD) and Secretary of Education to convene a panel of experts, known as the National Reading Panel in 2000, to identify effective instructional approaches in the teaching of reading due to concerns over the prevalence of students classified as learning disabled and participating in special education across states (Reschely and Hosp, 2004) and the overclassification of minority students as cognitively deficient or emotionally disturbed.	The National Backdrop Behind Student Achievement: President George W. Bush enacts the 2002 No Child Left Behind (NCLB) federal legislation, defining school accountability through the following policy mandates: • Standardized achievement testing is expanded to include all students in grades three through eight with few exemptions based on special education or second-language learner status. • Performance for all students on standardized tests is reported with the goal of achieving AYP (adequate yearly progress) for each subgroup of students (special education, second-language learners, race/ethnicity, and low income status). • SINI (School in Need of Improvement) status is used to identify any school for which subgroups did not achieve adequate yearly progress, imposing demands and sanctions of increasing severity for continued underperformance. • Charter schools and the restructuring of existing public schools are introduced to provide choice options for parents. • Based on findings of the National Reading Panel, essential components of reading instruction are identified under NCLB to include phonemic awareness, phonics, fluency, vocabulary, and text comprehension (K. Kemp, 2007).	The National Backdrop Behind Student Achievement: Transition from federal NCLB to President Obama's "Race to the Top" legislation with a focus on the following: • Higher performance expectations for students to ensure college and career readiness. • Federal funding awarded to states to develop technology systems for linking student achievement to teacher performance over time. • Exclusion from federal funding for states limiting growth in the number of charter schools. Common Core Standards Movement emerges promoting common core content knowledge and the application of higher-order cognitive skills to support student college and career readiness and regain a competitive edge for the United States in a global economy. Education policy pursues a "business model" (i.e., performance compensation, competition, value-added assessments) spawned by venture philanthropists such as Bill Gates and Sam Walton and the principles of marketing promulgated by statistician William Sanders. National economic crisis results in funding cuts to education and sparks a debate on entitlements, merit pay, and the role of teacher unions in school reform.

New York State Education Department Responses: State testing program is overhauled in 1999 and shifts test administration from grade three to grade four.

The Individuals with Disabilities Act is revised in 2004 to increase district and school accountability for the academic performance of students with disabilities.

New York State Education Department Responses: Expansion of testing to include grades three to five in 2005 to 2006 with student performance on state tests rated as below basic, basic, proficient, and advanced in reading and mathematics to comply with federal NCLB mandates.

Introduction of new testing policies in 2006 to 2007 to include all second-language learners (in an English-speaking school system for more than one year) and almost all special education students in the state testing program.

Dissemination and implementation of Response to Intervention (RTI) framework in 2007 requires districts and schools to provide tiered levels of services and interventions for struggling students and to monitor their progress through continuous data collection and analysis.

New York State Education Department Responses: Cut scores to achieve proficiency in ELA and mathematics on NYS assessments are raised in 2009 to 2010.

Content and format of state assessments are revised in length and rigor for grades three to eight in 2010 to 2011.

Initial dissemination and implementation of Common Core State Standards in schools and districts statewide.

Expansion of student performance tracking systems using technology to support implementation of new Annual Professional Performance Review (APPR) evaluation system with the goal of using student achievement data to determine part of the performance ratings of teachers and principals.

Grade	1996–1997	1997–1998	1998–1999	1999–2000	2000–2001	2001–2002	2002–2003	2003–2004	2004–2005	2005–2006	2006–2007	2007–2008	2008–2009	2009–2010	2010–2011
3 ELA	97%	95%	NA	NA	NA	NA	NA	NA	NA	95%	70%	65%	84%	30%	45%
4 ELA	NA*	NA	19%	61%	84%	85%	87%	82%	93%	98%	75%	70%	75%	49%	34%
5 ELA	NA	NA	NA	NA	NA	NA	NA	NA	NA	96%	67%	83%	83%	52%	63%
3 Math	100%	99%	NA	NA	NA	NA	NA	NA	NA	96%	90%	94%	99%	48%	67%
4 Math	NA	NA	75%	81%	85%	91%	99%	94%	94%	89%	89%	94%	84%	66%	41%
5 Math	NA	NA	NA	NA	NA	NA	NA	NA	NA	87%	92%	92%	95%	73%	76%

*NA (not applicable) indicates that a grade was not administered the state assessment for that particular school year.

special education and English Language Learners (ELL) would be included in testing cohorts. In classrooms throughout New York, special education students would be required to take all state assessments with the elimination of any IEP (Individualized Education Plan) accommodations on the ELA assessment that would compromise test integrity.

In addition, ELL students who had attended school in the United States "for a year and a day" would be required to take the state's ELA assessment with their English-proficient peers. These students would be granted extended time, where once they had been exempted from such testing for up to three years upon their arrival to allow the time necessary for the developmental acquisition of English as their second language.

Nearly all of Edison's students would be impacted by the many changes in testing and accountability prompted at the Exosystem and Macrosystem levels. In any given year, for example, approximately 44 percent of the total student population at Edison was considered ELL. Many of these students would be living from one day to the next with high rates of mobility within and across school districts, and outside of the country.

Although the percentages of special education students were much smaller than ELL learners by comparison, the full participation of both of these subgroups appeared to diminish the gains that had been demonstrated from 1999 to 2006. This time framework represented a period in which Edison had been highly recognized for its academic improvement by the NYS Education Department as a "High Achieving/Gap Closing School" and validated by them as a "Sharing Success Model" for its implementation of the community school strategy.

At the Exosystem and Macrosystem levels, substantive amendments to the state testing program were again enacted in the 2009 to 2010 and 2010 to 2011 school years, as part of the state's response to yet another national call for standards-based reform and accountability. The federal Race to the Top fund and the debates around reauthorization of the Elementary and Secondary Education Act (ESEA), still underway at the time of this writing, would establish higher standards for student performance in response to both public and corporate demands for American youth to be better able to compete academically with those of other nations participating in a global economy.

Race to the Top would seek to hold every level within education accountable for the improvement of student achievement and for providing support to students in need. Responding to these influences, the NYS Education Department modified its scoring rubric in 2009 to 2010 by raising the cut scores required to pass its assessments in ELA and mathematics and began plans to link principal and teacher evaluations to student achievement results. Raising the cut scores in 2009 to 2010 would negatively impact student achievement results in ELA and mathematics, not only for Edison but also for many schools across New York State and in other states receiving federal education funds.

In the interim, test results for ELL students at Edison taking state assessments in science and social studies in English or their native language, with the additional support of extended time, remained high and well above the eightieth percentile. However, New York State was forced to abandon its testing program in social studies in 2009 to 2010 as a cost-saving measure, a move reflecting the severe economic downturn taking place locally and nationally.

While continuing to require the higher performance levels established the year before, the state again modified the format and content of its assessments in reading and mathematics in 2010 to 2011, resulting in more challenging content and an expansion to a three-day test administration period for grades three and five (a three-day testing schedule had been confined to grade four prior to this time), with a tighter window for the completion of all state testing in the late spring. Despite these challenges, members of the Edison community continued in their determination to "rise to the occasion," using the strategic planning process and resources of the district and its partners to respond with results showing a number of trends toward improvement.

These complex and dramatic changes in the scale and format of annual testing make it difficult to track real progress in student achievement. However, the overall pattern we observed at Edison showed steady progress during periods when the same grades and cohort of students were tested using consistent measures. For example, after the state-mandated test changes in 1998 to 1999, fourth grade reading scores improved consistently until 2005 to 2006, when the next major testing change occurred. We believe that the community school strategy, with its array of targeted supports, contributed substantially to increased student achievement.

We also contend that this national push toward "raising the bar" has failed to take into consideration the rates of learning necessary for various subgroups of students to acquire challenging curriculum content. Given that current testing protocols may be inappropriate for students with significant learning challenges, and that it can take most ELL students from five to seven years to become competent enough to master and communicate academic content in a second language (Cummins, 1981), this push has prevented the public from stepping back to understand what teachers and students have been able to accomplish in what has truly been a turbulent world of accountability.

Regardless of the debate over the "legitimacy" or "feasibility" of the performance outcomes that have been established for students through federal legislation, leaders at all levels of schooling must respond and, as part of our work, we continue to advocate for the "one stop and engage all" approach that has been used effectively in community schools for more than a decade to help students succeed.

Educational practitioners will undoubtedly continue to struggle with meeting federal mandates in education and with finding ways in which to implement developmentally appropriate systems of assessment to measure both student progress and performance for years to come. Nevertheless, we answer the skeptics who raise the question regarding the need to establish community schools if there are no guarantees that this strategy will "immediately" or "permanently" result in higher test scores by arguing that it is essential to steer the course and remain all the more steadfast in one's commitment to supporting the needs of the whole child, despite and perhaps even because of the ever-changing contexts of education.

COMMUNITY SCHOOLS OUTCOMES SUPPORTING THE WHOLE CHILD

The evaluation of a community school can be facilitated by applying our definition of Whole Child Education to examining the impact of programs, services, and practices on one or more of the developmental domains of children's growth. Having provided an overview of student achievement data at Edison, the present section frames a discussion about community school outcomes in relation to the whole child. This discussion begins with an examination of available data related to the health and physical development of Edison students, and then moves on to examine other important outcomes related to their social-emotional, ethical, and intellectual development, each of which had been assisted through the school's partnerships.

Since the ecosystem of human development is constantly changing, extremely complex, and cannot be subject to the rigor or controls of scientific investigation, it is important to bear in mind that, although some research has incorporated a quasi-experimental or experimental design, most evaluation of community school outcomes is still based upon strong correlations between the data rather than in the establishment of direct causal relationships. In addition to assessing the result of planned or intended community school outcomes, it is helpful to consider the impact of any significant unplanned or unintended outcomes, as both can be equally as compelling.

The community school strategy at Edison, which represented a reform effort initiated at the school site with the district playing a support rather than coordinating role, required that each partner organization assume responsibility for the collection of data related to fulfilling their respective roles within the school. Edison's clearly defined organizational structure, as shown in figure 4.1, also created a mechanism by which any of the school's working subcommittees or Community School Advisory Board could request data that would serve to inform their decision making.

Although the school's efforts to collect data were complicated by the client or patient privacy codes that were maintained by all health and social service providers, Edison used both the quantitative and qualitative data that were available to its advantage. Qualitative data would often take the form of "illuminating" stories about the students and families behind the numbers and were used to document program effectiveness and garner support to sustain initiatives. Nevertheless, Edison's evaluation methods and procedures would have benefitted from the data collection systems already in place in districts where the community school strategy has been taken to scale.

THE OPEN DOOR FAMILY MEDICAL CENTERS
SUPPORTING HEALTHY PHYSICAL DEVELOPMENT

Since healthy physical development is fundamental to the community school's focus on the whole child, one of the earliest initiatives advocated for by the Edison Community School Advisory Board was the school-based health center. In collaboration with the Open Door Family Medical Centers and the office of Congresswoman Nita Lowey, the first school-based health centers were launched in 2004 at Edison and one additional district elementary school.

Information gathered by Open Door in 2002, during the initial planning phase, determined that only 23 percent of Edison students had health insurance and access to primary health care on a regular basis. The school-based health center was thus designed to assist with or to deliver the following: health insurance enrollment, primary care, immunizations and physicals, sick care visits, basic lab services, and nutrition guidance. When necessary, the center would also make mental and behavioral health referrals to other partners within the school or to off-site providers. From the moment it opened, between twenty-five to thirty-two students were seen daily for sick and wellness visits.

One of the benefits of the on-site medical services provided was reflected in the fact that 96 percent of the students seen on any given day were able to return to their classrooms and resume learning without disruption of the school day. Another important benefit of on-site access in the area of preventive care was best exemplified during the 2009 to 2010 public health crises over the H1N1 flu epidemic when nearly all of Edison students had been successfully vaccinated against this flu strain with not one child from the school being diagnosed with this illness.

School Day Programs, Services and Practices *"Building Community From the Inside Out and Creating a Culture of Excellence"*	After School and Summer Programs *"Promoting Full Integration Across Environments for Learning"*	Professional Development *"Building a Professional Learning Community"*	Edison Family Services *"Building Community From the Outside In Through Partnership"*
Underlying Principles • Develop a core values focus • Promote academic engagement through strong relational engagement • Provide integrated learning experiences to develop academic, social, emotional, and civic competencies • Create safe, inclusive, and supportive learning environments • Monitor and highlight both student performance and progress with a focus on continuous improvement	Underlying Principles • Reflect the school's core values • Promote academic engagement through strong relational engagement • Integrate academic and social skills development • Implement meaningful learning experiences • Monitor and highlight both student performance and progress with a focus on continuous improvement	Underlying Principles • Reinforce and model the school's core values as part of faculty and staff meetings, and at meetings involving parents and community members • Gain knowledge of ways to effectively implement Whole Child Education in the community school • Share best practices • Develop and sustain cross boundary leadership	Underlying Principles • Disseminate and engender commitment to the school's core values • Develop an understanding and commitment to Whole Child Education both in school and at home • Create a caring and inclusive school community • Support parents in their own roles as teachers, learners, advocates, and school leaders • Strive to have a positive impact on the surrounding community
School-wide Practices • Inter-grade Meetings • Town meetings • School unity builders (i.e. Family Math Night, Family Science Night, and publishing celebrations) • Service learning activities • Gallery Walk exhibition of student's thematic learning projects	After School Programs • Performing arts Modules • Book Club • One World Club- focus on global aspects of character education • "Prep for Success" small group tutoring sessions • SER "We Care After School Program" (homework help, sports and enrichment)	Edison/Manhattanville College PDS Partnership • On-site graduate courses • Faculty mentoring • Pre-service teacher education • Reading Reform Foundation Initiative-Training participating teachers in Reading Reform strategies	Family Engagement Opportunities • Topical workshops and seminars (bilingual) • "Second Cup of Coffee" weekly parent group • "EPIC (Every Person Influences Children) Family Literacy Program" • "Common Sense Parenting" course • School-wide health and wellness activities • PTA/District activities

Classroom Practices
- "Child Development Project" and "Responsive Classroom" strategies
  -Class meetings
  -Buddy classes
  -Developmental discipline
- Service learning projects

Small Group Counseling-Behavioral Intervention and Social Skills Curriculum
- "Second Step" Program delivered by school psychologist

Mental Health and Medical Services Offered by Community School Partners During the School Day
- Individual therapeutic counseling provided by the Guidance Center
- Open Door School-Based Health Center

After School Reading Practicum
- Manhattanville College provides individual tutoring sessions by its graduate level students in education

"Home Run Summer Program"
- Pre-service teachers from Manhattanville College serve as program coaches
- Integration of academic skills and character development as part of theme-based learning

Mental Health and Medical Services Offered by Community School Partners After School Hours
- Individual therapeutic counseling provided by the Guidance Center
- Open Door School-Based Health Center

Literacy Consultant Training
- Balanced Literacy- ELA strategies that differentiated instruction, developed student autonomy, and created a community of readers and writers

Character Education and Inclusive Classroom Practices
- Child Development Project and Responsive Classroom Training
- Training in Marilyn Friend Co-teaching Model

Professional Development on Health Related Topics Offered by Community School Partners:
- Guidance Center and Open Door-Topical presentations on bullying, child health issues, and the impact of adverse childhood experiences

Support and Empowerment of the Surrounding Community
- Community Health Fairs
- Housing Summits
- "Edison's Closet" – scheduled distribution of free clothing to families in need

Special Family Network Meetings (Facilitated by district and chaired by community school coordinator)
- "School-based Wrap Around Network"-relevant county agencies gather at parent request to assist in meeting their needs

Programs and Services for Parental Support and Empowerment Offered by Community School Partners
- Case Management services by the Guidance Center
- BOCES adult education programs (Spanish and English GED and English as a Second Language courses)
- Special Parenting Program- Hospital affiliated and delivered by the Guidance Center for parents of behaviorally challenging students

Figure 4.1. Edison's Organizational Structure. **"Committed to Community, Character and Academic Excellence"**

As part of Edison's commitment to providing a healthy educational eco-system for all its members, staff from the Open Door worked closely with the school and other partners to promote healthy environments both at home and in school and to strengthen the relationship between the two. Its first steps in this process included monitoring its own-efforts to improve the quality of the services delivered at the school-based health center, promote the health and wellness of the entire school community, and positively impact school health policies. The annual completion of the School-based Health Index (SBHI) would serve to guide this work.

The SBHI developed by the Centers for Disease Control includes a twenty-five-question survey that examines physical activity, healthy eat-ing, tobacco prevention, and school health policies in terms of strengths and weaknesses. The Open Door staff in collaboration with the school's Fit Kids Committee collected and analyzed data from this instrument from 2004 to 2011. During this period, the data consistently indicated a high performance score of over 80 percent beginning in the 2004 to 2005 school year, increasing steadily to 92.4 percent in 2008 to 2009 and reaching 95 percent in 2010 to 2011.

Results of the SBHI were used by Open Door and the Fit Kids Commit-tee to implement a variety of valuable programs, services, and activities that would benefit students, families, and staff as follows:

- Community Health Fair events held at the school site;
- The Fit Kids Open Airways Program involving regularly scheduled work-shops for students focusing on asthma management and increased knowl-edge about the value of exercise and good nutrition;
- Schoolwide health awareness activities including "No Junk Food Week" and an established calendar of health-related activities for children that was distributed to teachers and parents monthly;
- In-class lessons on flu prevention, personal hygiene, healthy snacking, and dental care for all grade levels and puberty education for fifth graders;
- Exercise programs tailored to the needs and interests of students, families, and staff (i.e., integrating walking into a daily routine, Zumba classes, and kindergarten aerobics);
- Parent/community presentations, including such topics as handling stress, cooking nutritionally balanced foods, and taking a smoke-free home pledge.

Since childhood obesity and asthma have emerged as major health risks for children throughout the country, with students living in poverty often suffer-ing more severe consequences for these conditions due to their limited access to good nutrition and quality health care, the Open Door began to assess and address these risk factors almost immediately upon opening the school-based center.

The Open Door began to monitor the Body Mass Index (routinely referred to as the BMI) of all enrolled students and offered its clinical expertise and guidance to those identified as being dangerously overweight, extending support to their parents as well. Open Door's nurse practitioner (colocated within the school) and pediatrician, both of whom had come to know the children and their families quite well, saw students regularly. Moreover, both parent and child would also benefit from consultation with Open Door's nutritionist and from schoolwide activities to promote healthy eating and overall wellness. As a result, Edison and Open Door would have reason to celebrate when it was determined that from 2005 to 2010 the number of students classified as obese had decreased by close to 50 percent, with the number of students classified at a healthy weight nearly doubling.

A further discovery by Open Door revealed that 15 percent of Edison students were suffering from asthma in 2004 to 2005, with only 2 percent of this group having asthma action plans completed by a physician or nurse practitioner. Consistent follow-up care for these students by staff from the school-based health center, complemented by workshops for these youngsters and their parents, resulted in the percentage of students being effectively managed (as determined by the completion of an asthma action plan by the nurse practitioner) for their condition increasing dramatically to 100 percent by 2010 to 2011.

One of the proudest achievements for the Open Door Family Medical Centers and the Thomas Edison Elementary School was to determine that the opening of its school-based health center would dramatically increase student access to health insurance coverage from 23 percent in 2002 to 2003, to 88 percent in 2005 to 2006, to 99 percent in 2010 to 2011. This pioneering partnership would also witness the replication of school-based health centers in three of the four district elementary schools, the middle school, and eventually the high school, an outcome that would benefit the entire Port Chester community.

The mission of the Open Door Family Medical Centers has been to provide quality health care and outreach to the medically underserved of the community. Advancing this organizational mission would be greatly facilitated by the placement of a school-based health center within the Thomas Edison Elementary School. Similarly, Open Door's presence would help Edison realize its own mission to provide support services to students in order to facilitate their well-being and, thus, their learning. Their relationship, so positively impacting the developmental domain of health and wellness in children, would underscore the reciprocal benefits to those organizations engaged in partnership within a community school.

THE GUIDANCE CENTER SUPPORTING
FAMILIES AND THE SOCIAL, EMOTIONAL,
AND ETHICAL DEVELOPMENT OF STUDENTS

The Guidance Center, Edison's mental health provider, began its partnership early in Edison's transformation into a community school, bringing to the forefront their deep knowledge of mental health issues facing poor, immigrant children in Westchester County. This organization, with the support of special federal grants awarded to the district and sometimes used in combination with county, state, foundation, and philanthropic funding, colocated the services of a full-time, bilingual caseworker and therapeutic social worker at the school site four to five days per week.

While the social worker provided therapeutic counseling to children in crisis, the caseworker's responsibilities included conducting general family outreach and parent education, assisting any family in need of securing social or mental health services (at the local, county, and state levels) and helping them obtain information about the school and the district. The caseworker was also charged with maintaining an assigned caseload of about twenty-five families in need of more intense and sustained intervention.

The view that enhancing family engagement is a means to improving a student's attitude, adjustment, and performance in school resonated well with the Guidance Center and formed an integral component of their work at Edison. Both the social worker and the caseworker provided various venues, during the day and in the evenings, for meetings with families in which a broad spectrum of relevant topics were covered. For example, workshops and presentations included publishing the immigration stories of parents so they could be shared with their children and addressing parents' concerns about puberty and adolescent sexuality. Each and every topic for these meeting had been identified by the parents themselves, by school personnel, or by experts in the field of mental health.

Participation in parent education programs would range from twenty to forty adult family members each month, with one group of approximately ten to fifteen parents and guardians meeting steadily each week as part of an informal group called the "Second Cup of Coffee" (*La Segunda Taza de Cafe* in Spanish).

The data demonstrated that at least 350 families per year had benefitted from the Guidance Center's collaboration with the Thomas Edison Elementary School, with well over three thousand parents and guardians participating in jointly sponsored parent education programs over the course of a decade. Those in attendance consistently reported (through evaluation surveys) that the information they received had been helpful to them and provided a greater understanding of the topics presented, thus encouraging the further expansion of family engagement initiatives.

In 2005, a six-week course on effective parenting was introduced by the district and conducted by the caseworker and two members of the school's faculty. The course was offered after the caseworker and faculty participants had been trained by the Boys Town Organization, using their "Common Sense Parenting" curriculum, which had received recognition from the National Parenting Center and the endorsement of many mental health professionals. Course content was specifically designed for parents facing a myriad of challenges and was particularly beneficial to families in need of learning different ways to discipline their children.

Through their participation, parents learned strategies for handling defiant behavior and general discipline. They also found ways to help their children exhibit better self-control and improve their decision-making and problem-solving abilities. From 2005 to 2011, feedback from "Common Sense Parenting" course participants indicated that the vast majority (from 85 percent to 100 percent) of those surveyed were completely satisfied with its content and felt that it had a positive impact on their family. Offered twice per year with approximately ten parents per semester (including fathers, mothers, grandparents, and guardians), this course was deemed so worthwhile that it continued to be offered through the years at Edison and at other elementary schools within the district, thereby substantiating both the need and value of this type of parent education.

The therapeutic social worker from the Guidance Center provided individual counseling to students in a designated space within the school building that had been approved for such purposes by the state's office of mental health. The therapist saw an average of thirty-five students annually, and the most commonly cited diagnoses for these cases included stress, anxiety, and depression. Treating the students would invariably involve offering secondary or colateral support to the family unit and, whenever necessary, referring them for more intense treatment to the Guidance Center's primary clinical facility or to the services of other community organizations.

Disorders exhibited by students involved in therapeutic counseling were frequently a by-product of the acute effects of their poverty and manifested through visible signs of strain within the child and the family unit. Stress, anxiety, and depression were frequently associated with any one or combination of the following: tenuous immigration status, homelessness, critical illness, spousal/child abuse, drug/alcohol abuse, and difficulties with learning and adjustment to the school setting.

Over more than a decade, the Guidance Center's therapists treated over 420 students. Recent results have shown more than half of the clients involved in counseling demonstrated improvement on the CANS-MH Assessment, an assessment used by child welfare agencies to screen and assess mental health and or social-emotional functioning in children.

Unlike most mental health agencies working in isolation from the school, the Guidance Center successfully used the community school setting to expand its work from individual counseling to enhancing the capacity of an entire educational ecosystem. The work of this organization, and the efforts of its caseworker, resulted in the successful recruitment of parents for the school's PTA, their increased participation in special school activities including parent-teacher conferences, and in their taking the first steps to broader district and community involvement.

The Guidance Center's programs would also pave the way for parents to become interested in furthering their own education and to become motivated to seek better employment opportunities, with one such parent being hired to serve in the role of parent coordinator in a neighboring school. The available evidence thus points to the power of community schools and their partners to encourage parental involvement, based upon a continuum that takes into account their needs and interests, readiness to serve at various levels of involvement (for example, as advocates for their own children or leaders within the school district), and availability (for example, by staff and partners offering to conduct home visits and schedule school programs flexibly).

We believe that there was a strong correlation between the programs and services provided to students and families through Edison's mental health partnership with the Guidance Center and the significant drop in disciplinary referrals that the school had seen over the years. Aimed at prevention and intervention, these programs and services produced a marked decrease in the percent of disciplinary referrals from 30 percent in 1996 to 1997 to 9 percent in 2010 to 2011, with the number of students suspended remaining relatively low, at about 2 percent per year, despite significant increases in student enrollment.

We also conclude that the drop in disciplinary referrals, further supported by the school's strong emphasis on character education, reflected an improvement in the self-esteem of students and the "more ethical choices" they had learned to make with regard to the treatment of others and to respecting school property and the personal property of others.

MANHATTANVILLE COLLEGE SUPPORTING THE ACADEMIC GROWTH OF STUDENTS AND THE PROFESSIONAL DEVELOPMENT OF TEACHERS

An essential ingredient to successfully implementing any school reform strategy is to gain both the endorsement and commitment of the school's faculty, and Edison's connection with Manhattanville College enabled the teachers to immediately experience the benefits of partnership. It is important to point out that this relationship grew incrementally over the years, with the college first participating in the community school planning process from 1996 to 1998. Their involvement continued with the introduction of student teachers and site-based courses from 2001 to 2003 and culminated in the official ribbon-cutting ceremony that launched the college's first PDS relationship in 2002 to 2003.

Since its inception, teachers readily endorsed PDS partnership initiatives because they were well integrated into a community school design that clearly benefitted children and families, as well as their own growth as professionals. As shown earlier in figure 1.2, Edison conceptualized its community school model as a "one stop" center on two levels, one providing targeted support for families, and the other assisting student learning in a variety of ways. Preservice teacher candidates were involved at both levels, helping teachers and community partners conduct parent education and providing direct instruction to students.

From 2001 to 2011, approximately 160 students at Edison benefitted from the services of eight to ten student teachers each year with approximately eighty classrooms and 1,600 students being served over a ten-year period. When surveyed, Edison students enthusiastically acknowledged that having a student teacher in their classroom had "given them different ways to learn, gotten more of their school work accomplished, allowed them to participate in more special projects, and given them more individual attention."

Over the same ten-year period, classroom instruction was successfully supplemented by preservice teacher candidates involved in site-based courses held during the school day. Their efforts would cumulatively translate into more than six hundred students and twenty-four Edison classrooms being served in the areas of literacy, special education, social studies, and science. Data gathered over a two-year period related to one such site-based course in special education indicated that 100 percent of students receiving tutoring as part of its design demonstrated improvement in word recognition, as measured by district literacy assessments used for progress monitoring, as well as on pretesting and posttesting measures conducted at the end of each semester.

Moreover, the literacy practicum held as part of after-school programming also demonstrated a significant impact on the literacy skills of at-risk learners receiving individual tutoring from course participants. These graduate-level course participants, who were often practicing teachers, were able to give a fresh perspective on the students they tutored as well as implement the new strategies they had learned as part of their studies. Their impact was apparent, with approximately 75 percent of the ninety-four students involved from

2002 to 2011 achieving the required level of proficiency on state assessments in ELA.

In Edison's community school design, the professional development afforded to teachers was also conceived of as a level of support for student learning. Edison teachers overwhelmingly reported through survey data and focus group sessions (for example, mentoring meetings, PDS Committee discussions, and meetings with teachers supervising student teachers) the value of the professional development offered to them and the exposure to new instructional strategies they had received through the PDS partnership. For this reason, we strongly recommend a similar approach when initiating a school-university partnership and planning for the implementation of a community school.

Since initiating both site-based and college-campus course options for Edison faculty at a free or reduced rate in 2003, 33 percent of Edison teachers were able to obtain advanced certifications or an additional masters degree in areas such as teaching English as a second language, educational administration, and teacher leadership. Equally as impressive, 11 percent of Edison's full-time professional staff, including the principal, had acted in the capacity of adjunct faculty and coauthored professional articles with college professors, with several serving as guest presenters at seminars and symposia offered by the college or at national conferences.

For Manhattanville College, its goal of community outreach and its commitment to diversity were easily realized by embedding a PDS relationship within a community school. For Edison, the outcomes described provide solid evidence of measurable academic progress for students and evidence, equally as strong, of growth in teacher skills and knowledge. The community school thus represents the ideal setting for professional learning experiences that are highly relevant, for both teachers and those preparing to enter the profession, and profoundly connected to promoting a real understanding of Whole Child Education.

EXTERNAL VALIDATION AND THE
THOMAS EDISON ELEMENTARY SCHOOL

The Thomas Edison Elementary School was fortunate to have been selected for a number of important validation and research studies from 1999 to 2009 as a result of its improvement in student achievement, inclusive school practices, and for its highly successful community school initiatives. In a study commissioned in 2002 by the Sharing Success Program of the New York State Education Department, an independent researcher examined student achievement data at Edison for the purpose of validating and disseminating the strategies that had been implemented.

The research examined the percentage of students at or above the level 3 performance standard on state assessments and the mean score in ELA and mathematics from 1999 to 2001. After a thorough review of state reporting data, a visit to the school by the independent researcher, and a presentation to State Education Officials by staff and community representatives, Edison received recognition as a Sharing Success dissemination model. The research would conclude that leadership with a strong commitment to professional development and the integration of community resources had successfully turned around the culture of the school and subsequently the test scores.

In 2009, a site visitation team, composed of a select group of experts in the field of special education, came to Edison to conduct a review of student achievement data, the instructional practices of the coteaching model implemented, and the support services offered to families. As a result of a rigorous process that included interview discussions with school staff and parents, Edison's inclusive school practices and integrated networks of support for children and families were highly commended and led to the school receiving a STAIR Dissemination Award by the U.S. Department of Education.

External validation would attract many visitors to Edison over the years, both from neighboring districts and from other regions across the country. As a result of its firmly established reputation as a community school, Edison would eventually come to host a number of international visitors as well.

In addition to using the results of external validation to document how leadership and collaboration had worked at Edison to support children and families, it is equally as important to assess how community school initiatives are seamlessly integrated to form a cohesive educational ecosystem. This task may be particularly difficult for community school practitioners, whose focus on data collection has been mainly to assess the impact of programs, services, and practices on student achievement and not necessarily to assess how well these networks of support work together. For Edison, the role of an external researcher, oriented to the ecology of human development, proved to be extremely valuable in this endeavor.

From 2004 to 2007, Edison became the focus of a research study conducted by New York University's Metropolitan Center for Urban Education as a result of having been identified for dramatically improving student achievement by the New York State Education Department. The research methods for the study included a thorough examination of student achievement data and a qualitative analysis of information gathered from focus group discussions with key stakeholders and from capturing the school in action through classroom observations.

Their research used the term *synergy* to describe the structural bonds that existed across the partner networks at Edison and pointed out that these elements have been frequently lacking in school partnerships. These structural bonds were identified as common values, a common language, and common reflective practice and were found to be sustained by the conditions of common physical space, community trust, and leadership (Martin, Fergus, and Noguera, 2010) found within the school. In writing this book, we have revisited these research findings and have noted many examples of the synergy and structural bonds they describe in our own portrayals and explanations of the following:

- A conceptual framework of Whole Child Education that was linked to a shared vision of a community school;
- A common language for literacy instruction, discipline, and character education developed within the school;
- Instructional practices and school culture that deliberately incorporated community building and self-reflection;
- A strategic focus on results and continuous improvement;
- An intentional focus on team building, cross-boundary leadership, and productive group work;
- Flexibility and shared use of personnel, resources, and space;
- A "One Stop, Engage All" community school design.

Case study findings led the researchers to conclude that integrative networks of support for children, families, and teachers, together with enriched and expanded opportunities for learning and strong relational engagement, have tremendous power to counteract the effects of poverty in ways that will ultimately serve to improve student learning. They conclude that the community school is the ideal setting for creating these types of structures and interactions.

Many noteworthy findings have been derived from the validation and research studies conducted at the Thomas Edison Elementary School. In addition, a conceptual framework for collaborative leadership has been developed by Wepner (Wepner and Hopkins, 2011), using Edison as an example of this type of leadership. In doing so, Wepner introduces the term *entrepreneurial leadership* to identify the means by which Edison was able to set into motion a partnership vision that would bring the community into the building each day to support new ways of doing business. Her conceptual framework would suggest similar themes as those in the findings of earlier studies.

As a result of Edison's successful implementation of school-linked services and Whole Child Education, state and federal funding streams continued to be made available to the district through the advocacy efforts of legislators at all levels interested in sustaining, replicating, and expanding these initiatives. In turn, district personnel became extremely adept at strategically blending such funding streams with those made available through competitive grants and other resources to not only continue their support of Edison but also to expand community school strategies to several other schools within the district. Clearly, replication and longevity may perhaps be considered the best indicators of validation for the community school as a reform strategy.

EDISON RESULTS IN A NATIONAL CONTEXT

Edison's planning team faced many of the challenges that have confronted other community schools—changing baselines, changing benchmarks, changing demographics, confidentiality, attribution issues, and many others. And, like many colleagues in the field, the Edison team thought broadly about success indicators for students, families, and the school itself—attendance, behavior, academic progress, parental engagement, teacher effectiveness, and health care access, among others. These results are consistent with the formalized framework developed by leaders of the field, who worked together as part of the Coalition for Community Schools to agree on a comprehensive set of outcomes that could guide the field in its efforts to produce and document results. This framework outlines five short-term results of community schools:

- Children are ready to enter school;
- Students attend school consistently;
- Students are actively involved in learning and in their community;
- Families are increasingly involved in their children's education;
- Schools are engaged with families and communities.

The framework also indicates four long-term results that community schools should seek to effect:

- Students succeed academically;
- Students are healthy—physically, socially, and emotionally;
- Students live and learn in safe, supportive, and stable environments;
- Communities are desirable places to live.

During these same years that the Edison planning team was transforming its school into a community school and documenting its results, the national field was producing similar and additional results that help to make the collective case for working in this more comprehensive and integrated way. Some community school initiatives received external funding and were able to commission third-party evaluations, using quasi-experimental and even experimental designs; others relied on university partners or district data systems, and many paid concerted attention to existing sources of school and partner data, as did the Edison team.

EVALUATION IN COMMUNITY SCHOOLS ACROSS THE COUNTRY

The following is a brief summary of several of these studies, arranged chronologically in an effort to show the evolution of the field's thinking and approach.

The Children's Aid Society

After opening its first community school in New York City in 1992, this organization commissioned a quasi-experimental study conducted by a collaborative team from Fordham University's graduate schools of education and social services. The initial study, conducted from 1993 to 1996, focused on four schools: two Children's Aid Society (CAS) community schools, one at the elementary level and the other, a middle/intermediate school; and two carefully matched comparison schools.

Steady progress in reading and math was documented at the CAS community schools during the period from 1993 to 1996. At the CAS middle school (I.S. 218), math performance increased from 37 percent of students at grade level in 1994, to 44 percent in 1995, to 51 percent in 1996—a total change of nearly 40 percent over two years. In the third-grade cohort that entered the CAS elementary school (P.S. 5) in 1993, only 10.4 percent of students were reading at grade level. In that same cohort, 16.2 percent of students were reading at grade level by the fourth grade, and 35.4 percent by the fifth grade. Math achievement at P.S. 5 increased from 23.4 percent at grade level in the third-grade class in 1993, to 32.1 percent in fourth grade, to 56 percent in fifth grade.

Later evaluations showed that students at I.S. 218 and P.S. 5 continued to improve in math and reading scores. The Fordham team analyzed Board of Education data related to student achievement on the California Achievement Test (CAT) in mathematics and the CBT Reading Test (Brickman, Cancelli, and Sanchez, 1998).

The Fordham studies also showed higher student and teacher attendance at the community schools, compared to the control schools; considerably more parental engagement; better school climate; and increased neighborhood safety and reduced neighborhood violence around the community schools (Clark and Engle, 2000).

Subsequent evaluations have documented other positive findings, such as greater academic gains for after-school participants in CAS community schools compared to nonparticipants (Clark et al., 2008), and better attendance and greater academic progress at CAS community schools compared to all New York City schools and to peer schools (Clark et al., 2009). Another study found that students with serious mental health problems were able to stay on track academically when given regular access to high-quality mental health services (Clark and Engle, 2003).

Communities in Schools

In 2005, this national organization commissioned a rigorous five-year national longitudinal evaluation with an independent outside evaluator (ICF International) to understand the effectiveness of its model and under what conditions the impact of Communities in Schools was the greatest. The Communities in Schools (CIS) model, which operates in 3,400 schools located in twenty-five states, includes the active engagement of a school-based coordinator who organizes all of the following student support services at each school site:

- Comprehensive school- and student-level needs assessments;
- Annual school- and student-level plans for delivery of prevention and intervention services;
- Community asset assessment and identification of service partners;
- Delivery of appropriate and responsive services to students;
- Data collection and evaluation for reporting and modification of service strategies.

The multimethod evaluation (ICF International, 2010) produced impressive results, especially in schools that maintained fidelity to the CIS service delivery model; these results included decreased dropout rates, increased graduation rates, academic achievement as measured by math and reading proficiency levels in selected grades, improved student behavior, and improved student attendance.

City Connects

This initiative is a school-based intervention in seventeen urban elementary schools in Boston. A partnership between the Boston Public Schools, Boston

College, and a variety of community resources, City Connects places a full-time student support professional in each school, who works with teachers and others to assess the strengths and needs of every student in key areas of development, including but not limited to academic achievement. The coordinator then helps identify a unique support plan for each student and connects the student to a set of tailored support services. The coordinator also develops partnerships with community agencies to secure needed services and enrichment opportunities, tracks the support plan electronically for each student, and follows up to assure service delivery and effectiveness.

The partners at Boston College created a rigorous evaluation design that allows for comparison of academic achievement and other outcomes between City Connects students and other Boston Public School students. The evaluators found the beneficial effects of City Connects on academic achievement to be "significant and lasting." For example, after leaving City Connects in fifth grade, students outperform their Boston peers in middle school and achieve close to state proficiency levels on both English and math on the Massachusetts statewide test (MCAS).

City Connects has also demonstrated lasting improvements in report card scores for academic achievement. Despite starting with lower report card scores at the beginning of first grade, City Connects students surpass those in comparison schools, demonstrating higher scores in all subject areas by the end of the fifth grade. This evaluation also documented other positive outcomes, including behavior, attendance, and health care access (Boston College Center for Child, Family and Community Partnerships, 2010).

Cincinnati Public Schools Community Learning Centers

The Cincinnati initiative was launched districtwide in 2001 in response to the growing need to provide supports for community reinvestment in public schools, neighborhood revitalization, and the healthy development of "whole" students and their families. Understanding that student success is contingent on parental and community support, the Community Learning Centers (CLC) model was designed not only to provide academic reinforcements for students but also to develop community-centered "hubs" that provide resources for neighborhood residents through colocated partnerships. Services include tutoring, mentoring, after-school enrichment, college access, parent and family engagement, and health/wellness services.

Most of the now fifty-eight CLCs have a Resource Coordinator, whose role is to integrate school-day and extended-day learning and to connect students and families to needed services. Cincinnati has led the way nationally for data sharing between its school system and community partners, and the

Resource Coordinators also carry responsibility for making sure that student-level records are maintained regularly and accurately. A new data dashboard has created linkages between school and community partnership data and has allowed the CLC's external evaluator to document impressive results in 2011:

- *Partners are being engaged in the schools to meet student needs:* During the 2010 to 2011 academic school year, 322 partners provided academic, mentoring, college access, after-school, health-wellness, mental health, parent and community engagement initiatives and other services;
- *Students with needs are being linked to services:* Data show that the majority of students with unmet needs are being identified and linked to individual services as a result of targeted resource coordination;
- *Students receiving resource coordination services show positive academic trends and other positive outcomes:* Although targeted students tend to have greater unmet needs than other students, those receiving resource coordination services showed positive academic trends on state standardized tests (OAA) and other outcomes (attendance, punctuality, behavior) compared to students not receiving those services;
- *High rates of parent engagement and parent volunteering:* Resource Coordinators found high levels of parent participation in the Community Learning Centers, with more than half of parents actively engaged in their children's learning (Mitchell, 2011).

Hartford Community Schools

Another external evaluation that has documented positive results of community schools is taking place in Hartford (Connecticut), where the OMG Center for Collaborative Learning has tracked the progress of students in five community schools for the past three years. The initiative is the result of a partnership between the Hartford Public Schools, the Hartford Office of Youth Services (a city department), the Hartford Foundation for Public Giving, and the local United Way. The evaluation is documenting progress at three levels: systems-building, school-level efforts, and progress toward outcomes.

To date, the evaluation has been able to track positive student outcomes in several areas, including math and reading achievement. Although reading proficiency levels were lower across community schools at baseline than across all Hartford schools, this pattern shifted in 2010, with a greater percentage of community school students scoring proficient or above on the Connecticut Mastery Test in reading. In addition, students who participated in the after-school portion of community schools showed gains across all the areas tested statewide (reading, writing, math). Although this initiative and evaluation do not have the longevity of the others cited, these results are included because they show great promise at an early stage of the work.

Other Evaluations

Finally, the Coalition for Community Schools conducted and published a summary of existing community schools evaluations in 2009, titled *Community Schools Research Report 2009*. Citing evaluation findings from across the country (Chicago, Cincinnati, Des Moines, Los Angeles, New York City, Philadelphia, San Mateo County, Tukwila, Washington, and others), this report noted:

> A growing body of research suggests that fidelity to the community schools strategy yields compounding benefits for students, families and the community. Community school students show significant gains in academic achievement and in essential areas of nonacademic development. Families of community school students show increased family stability, communication with teachers, school involvement, and a greater sense of responsibility for their children's learning. Community schools enjoy stronger parent-teacher relationships, increased teacher satisfaction, a more positive school environment, and greater community support. The community school model promotes more efficient use of school buildings and, as a result, neighborhoods enjoy increased security, heightened community pride, and better rapport among students and residents. (Coalition for Community Schools, 2009)

The state of evaluation in the community schools field has developed so rapidly over the past decade that the Children's Aid Society was able to sponsor a national conference on the topic during the fall of 2011. In addition to sharing their results and methodologies with one another in workshop sessions, participants explored the many technical issues involved in assessing results of complex comprehensive interventions like community schools—issues like sharing data across multiple systems, understanding confidentiality laws such as the Family Educational Rights and Privacy Act (FERPA) and HIIPA, selecting an external evaluator, and creating a theory of change.

The next stage of this work will involve creating common indicators that community school practitioners across the country will agree to measure. The Coalition for Community Schools has taken a leadership role in convening the field around this effort, building on its earlier work to summarize results to date and to collect and publish evaluation instruments in an *Evaluation Toolkit.*

CHAPTER SUMMARY

In this chapter, an ecological perspective was used to frame the evaluation processes in the community school. We began by fully acknowledging that these processes are difficult because the data is highly correlational and so much more complex and multifaceted than in the traditional school setting, where the primary indicator of success will ultimately be determined on the basis of results on standardized tests of student achievement. Admittedly, community schools also bear this responsibility; however, the broader outcomes they examine offer a more comprehensive view of school effectiveness.

Several ways to approach evaluation in the community school setting were described, beginning with the application of our working definition of Whole Child Education to an examination of outcomes based on one or more of the developmental domains of children's growth and learning. In doing so, we shared the efforts of the Thomas Edison Elementary School to focus on results and continuous improvement and to document the outcomes that resulted from its partnerships.

A case study of Edison, conducted by a well-known research university, was also examined because of its unique approach to integrating an ecological perspective as part of an analysis of student literacy achievement and school transformation. Their work is important as it provides a thoughtful investigation of the structures and interactions necessary for the effective implementation of a community school and provides further validation of the exceptional bond between theory and practice that has been a prevalent theme throughout the book.

What we have learned from Edison's experiences with evaluation and from looking at community schools in different parts of the country, where districts have taken the community school strategy to scale, is that these efforts have certainly extended their reach beyond the classroom to look closely at how these schools are able to rally an entire educational ecosystem in support of student learning.

The evaluation methods and studies included in the discussion give educational practitioners insights about the impact of community schools on a number of student success indicators, including, for example, attendance, discipline, behavior, and adjustment to school. They also bring to light the potential of the community school and its integrative networks to encourage parental involvement, enhance teacher skills and knowledge, and assist both the school and its partners in achieving their organizational missions. Moreover, research evidence has identified the ways in which community schools have positively impacted the surrounding neighborhood.

We conclude that the "big picture" of an emerging field of research and evaluation in community school settings has yielded very promising results. Descriptions of this research have illustrated the ways in which one particular school and several large school districts have developed systems for the collection and organization of meaningful data across a range of indicators; however, experts acknowledge that this field of evaluation represents an area for future exploration and growth.

Chapter Five

Sustaining the Community School

Sustainability is often thought to mean one thing: fund-raising. But leaders in the community schools field—as well as in other arenas of social change—have adopted a more holistic and useful definition of sustainability, one that has been advanced by The Finance Project, a national organization based in Washington, D.C. According to The Finance Project (Langford and Flynn-Khan, 2003), sustainability of social innovations revolves around eight interrelated elements:

1. Vision: A clear statement about how an initiative's programs or activities will improve the lives of children, families, and communities;
2. Results Orientation: The ability to demonstrate program success through measurable results (for example, established indicators and performances measures);
3. Strategic Financing Orientation: The ability to identify the resources needed to sustain changed practices and activities, coupled with effective strategies that bring these resources together to achieve stated goals;
4. Adaptability to Changing Conditions: Adjusting to changing social, economic, and political trends in the community, taking advantage of new opportunities and identifying external threats that could obstruct program continuation;
5. Broad Base of Community Support: Cultivating relationships with stakeholders in the community who need the initiative and who would care if it were gone;
6. Key Champions: Rallying leaders from businesses, faith-based institutions, government, and other parts of the community who are committed to an initiative's vision and are willing to use their power and prestige to generate support for that program;

7. Strong Internal Systems: Building strong fiscal management, accounting, information, personnel systems, and governance structures, thus enabling an initiative to work effectively and efficiently, to document results, and to demonstrate soundness to potential funders;

8. Sustainability Plan: Creating a concrete written plan that specifies benchmarks around the scope and scale of service delivery, resources needed to ensure effective service delivery, financing targets, and resource prospects.

According to The Finance Project, sustainability planning is not a linear process, and these eight elements do not need to be developed in the sequence listed above. But all contribute to developing a complete picture and to achieving lasting change. At the Thomas Edison Elementary School, sustaining whole-child, whole-school education reform for fifteen years required attention to all eight elements, starting with a strong, shared vision.

Vision

As Anthony Bryk (2010) and other education researchers have found, strong principal leadership is often the key driver of school change and seems to work best when the principal has an inclusive leadership style. At Edison, the principal sought to transform a traditional public school into a community school in an effort to promote student success by addressing children's academic and nonacademic needs. She quickly recognized that she could not achieve this vision on her own—and she also recognized that her basic vision could be enhanced by the active participation of teachers, parents, and community partners.

The development of the Community School Advisory Board was a critical early decision that fostered shared leadership and collective trust. As was described in chapter 2, developing an explicit and compelling shared vision among all the partners constituted an essential step in transforming Edison into a community school.

Results Orientation

Edison's Community School Advisory Board also took responsibility for articulating a broad set of results for which it would hold itself responsible. In keeping with the community schools philosophy and approach, these results included but went beyond academic proficiency; other important results included student attendance, behavior, physical and mental health, social and emotional skills, ethical development, and family well-being.

Strategic Financing Orientation

As outlined in chapter 2, under Core Competency #4, the Edison team thought broadly about how to identify, allocate, and combine a variety of resources that could support its comprehensive and integrated vision. This broad approach included making the best use of existing financial resources available to the schools (for example, Title I, III, and IV dollars)—a strategy that all schools can adopt immediately.

The Edison team's expansive approach to financing also involved enlisting the support of community partners whose expertise was aligned with the school's vision and could respond to the school's needs assessment; cultivating long-term relationships with elected officials; and applying, in collaboration with the district, for selected discretionary grant funds (such as the Full-Service Community Schools grant awards allocated through the U.S. Department of Education).

The Advisory Board recognized early on the importance of having diversified sources of support that combined public and private resources and that relied on in-kind as well as monetary contributions.

Adaptability to Changing Conditions

The Edison planning team and district leaders stayed attuned to changes in the larger policy and funding climate, in part because of its basic orientation to the operating context or "exosystem." Despite cutbacks in education funding at all levels, the Edison team benefitted from changes in Title I allowances, particularly from a 2010 modification of federal rules that now explicitly allow Title I funds to underwrite the salaries for Community School Directors. At Edison, the Community School Coordinator played an essential role as the principal's "go-to" person—recruiting and managing external partners, participating in joint planning, representing the community school at public and community events, responding to crises, trouble-shooting, and problem-solving.

But funding the coordinator's salary over the years has required creativity and commitment. For this reason, the recent changes in the Title I rules have constituted an important breakthrough for Edison and other community schools. In addition, by regularly monitoring Requests for Proposals from New York state and the federal government, the Edison team and the district's assistant superintendent for grants have been able to compete for 21st Century Community Learning Center dollars (federal funds that are administered by state departments of education) and for federal full-service community school resources.

Broad Base of Community Support

Because Edison saw itself as a cornerstone of the Port Chester community, its regular modus operandi involved participating in citywide events and in community coalitions, such as the Port Chester Cares Community Coalition. Its five strategic partners not only engaged in joint planning and the delivery of services at the school site but they also helped to build a broad base of support for the work of the community school by expanding its network and increasing its visibility.

Key Champions

The Edison leadership team cultivated a variety of important champions over the years. One of the school's key champions has been Congresswoman Nita Lowey, who has hosted high-level visits to the school, provided financial support, and discussed the work of the school in congressional speeches and media interviews. Other important champions have emerged from academia, including Harvard and New York Universities. As a community school, Edison was featured by the Harvard Full-Service Community Schools Roundtable and NYU's Metropolitan Center for Urban Education. Finally, as a full partner, Manhattanville College became a leading champion for Edison among its higher education and funding constituencies.

Strong Internal Systems

As a data-driven institution, Edison paid close attention to the development of strong internal systems that monitored all of its operations, including human and financial resources, and a broad set of outcomes, including academic, social, emotional, and physical. The Edison Community School Advisory Board regularly maintained oversight of operations and outcomes.

Sustainability Plan

A Strategic Action Plan (described fully in chapter 2) guided the partnership recruitment and management as well as the fund-raising aspects of Edison as a community school. This plan as indicated earlier evolved over time as the documented needs of the students and their families changed and as the operating context was modified.

EDISON'S INCLUSIVE LEADERSHIP: A KEY TO SUCCESS

One key lesson from the Edison experience of sustaining its comprehensive and integrated approach to public education for fifteen years was the essential role played by its planning team, the Thomas Edison Community School Advisory Board. This cross-boundary leadership group exemplifies the best thinking from both the Coalition for Community Schools (Blank et al., 2006) and The Finance Project (Langford and Flynn-Khan, 2003) about what it takes to institutionalize changed practice.

As noted in chapter 2, school improvement teams often rely entirely on school/district personnel and parents, whereas the Edison leadership team by design included all of its strategic community partners. These community partners brought not only a different knowledge base and skill set from those of professional educators but also different connections and networks, which can become key contributors to a community school's sustainability efforts.

SUSTAINING COMMUNITY SCHOOLS AND THE NATIONAL CONTEXT

Over the past few years, the community schools field has produced a growing body of knowledge about how to sustain this comprehensive, integrated approach to public education. The Children's Aid Society's National Center for Community Schools has developed a variety of resources, including case studies and training modules, which apply The Finance Project's basic ideas about sustainability planning to the work of community schools (National Center for Community Schools, 2011).

The Coalition for Community Schools published an excellent monograph titled *Financing Community Schools: Leveraging Resources to Support Student Success*, which draws on the experience of forty-nine mature community schools in seven cities. This publication offers general principles on financial sustainability and specific examples from a variety of individual community schools and from several multisite initiatives (Blank et al., 2010).

Finally, The Finance Project's *Sustainability Planning Workbook* is an essential tool for community school planners (Langford and Flynn-Khan, 2003). Divided into five modules, the workbook provides hands-on planning tools that guide users toward becoming concrete and specific about the scope and scale of what they want to sustain, including five critical financing strategies that they can use as they create their tailored sustainability plan.

As individual community schools and community school initiatives have applied these ideas, the field has learned a great deal about how to think broadly about financing strategies. For example, here are some specific ways that community school leaders have developed or leveraged financial resources, using the five critical financing strategies as a guide:

1. *Making the best possible use of existing resources (cash and in-kind contributions):* The Evansville-Vanderburgh School Corporation in Indiana stands out as a national exemplar of maximizing this financing strategy. Under the leadership of the associate superintendent for Family, School and Community Partnerships, Cathlin Gray, the district uses its community schools strategy to drive its resource development and allocation efforts (in contrast to many schools and districts that allow funding availability to drive their reform strategies).

   Dr. Gray and her team have used a savvy and creative approach in allocating available federal resources (such as Title I, IDEA, Even Start, and Head Start dollars) to their community school efforts, and in combining these federal funds with state and district resources to support the work outlined in their districtwide community schools plan.

2. *Tracking and maximizing available funding from public and private sources:* Evansville and other districts have also been successful in applying for competitive grants through a variety of federal sources (including Safe Schools/Healthy Students and Full-Service Community Schools grants) and combining these new dollars with existing resources to pursue ambitious districtwide approaches to community schools. Many community schools rely on 21st Century Community Learning Centers funding for their after-school and summer enrichment programs; these are competitive grants that are administered by state departments of education.

   Another excellent source of funds for community schools across the country is United Way. In some locales, such as Lehigh Valley (Pennsylvania) and Salt Lake City (Utah), the United Way has taken a lead role in developing and funding multisite community school initiatives. In other areas, such as Cincinnati (Ohio), Hartford (Connecticut), and Portland (Oregon), the United Way is a long-term funding partner. Community foundations are yet another private funding partner in many of these same cities.

3. *Identifying and pursuing opportunities to create more flexibility in existing categorical funding:* As cited earlier, recent changes in federal legislation have made it easier for local schools and districts to use Title I funds to support the work of community school coordinators. Another example of this strategy in action is the efforts of school-based health center advocates, in New York and other states, to request and gain increased flexibility in the use of Medicaid dollars—for example, to underwrite the provision of school-based mental health services by licensed social workers.

4. *Generating new resources by engaging public- and private-sector partners:* Many community schools have forged effective partnerships with area businesses, which often provide funding, corporate volunteers, and workplace internships. Often these partnerships create new champions for community schools. Media partners have included public television, public radio, and newspapers. Public partners can include municipal departments and county governments (both of which can align the work of libraries, parks, child welfare, juvenile justice, public health and mental health, and social services with the work of schools).

   Increasingly, community school initiatives are linking with higher education partners for a wide variety of purposes, including teacher preparation and development (as Edison did), research and evaluation support, placements for work-study students, and college access programming for middle and high school students.

5. *Advocating for new state and local revenue sources:* Several community school initiatives around the country—including Portland (Oregon) and San Francisco—benefit from children's tax levies that were approved by voters in those cities. Another excellent example of a new revenue source is a California ballot initiative several years ago that produced new revenues for mental health services by levying a special tax on the incomes of millionaires. Advocates in New York City have proposed a new tax on cell phone use that would benefit children's programs.

The current dilemma for most community school practitioners and advocates is how to support a comprehensive and integrated approach to education and youth development with the dizzying array of categorical and disjointed financial resources. As the above example indicates, practitioners on the ground have struggled mightily, and often successfully, to work within the existing parameters, while also advocating for the kinds of public policies and funding streams that are better aligned with the community schools strategy.

Both the longevity and the results of community schools have begun to influence state and national education policy. In New York State, the state's successful Race to the Top application to the U.S. Department of Education included a provision for full-service community schools, based in part on successful efforts like the Thomas Edison Elementary School in Port Chester and The Children's Aid Society's community schools in New York City. Similarly, federal education policy is becoming increasingly supportive of community schools, as seen in the recent changes in Title I eligibility rules as well as in several new provisions under discussion as part of the reauthorization of the Elementary and Secondary Education Act.

Chapter Six

A Call to Action: National Implications for Policy and Practice

A recent *New York Times* "op ed" article by an education professor (Helen Ladd) and a veteran education writer (Edward Fiske) observed:

> No one seriously disputes the fact that students from disadvantaged households perform less well in school, on average, than their peers from more advantaged backgrounds. But rather than confront this fact of life head-on, our policy makers mistakenly continue to reason that, since they cannot change the backgrounds of students, they should focus on things they can control. (December 12, 2011)

This article went on to note that "education policy makers should try to provide poor students with the social supports and experiences that middle class students enjoy as a matter of course"—high-quality early childhood, enriched learning during nonschool hours (after-school programs and summer camps), health and mental health services. The authors of this article are part of a growing chorus of education leaders and social justice advocates who have recognized the limitations of America's current education policies—policies that increase accountability for schools and teachers without increasing opportunities for students to learn.

The 2002 passage of the federal No Child Left Behind legislation set in motion a variety of accountability measures that call for all children to be proficient in the core academic subjects by 2014. Most of the ensuing reforms focused solely on instructional quality: adoption of state-level academic standards; curricular improvements; teacher quality; principal leadership; and alignment of assessments to curricula. More controversial aspects of these reforms include efforts to end teacher tenure, to promote merit pay for teachers, and to link teacher effectiveness measures with student performance.

But precious few of the efforts spawned by NCLB have paid serious attention to the learner side of the teaching-and-learning equation. While instructional quality is certainly a necessary component of education reform, many experts—including practitioners, researchers, and advocates—recognize that, by itself, instructional quality is an insufficient remedy if America is going to truly address its achievement gap.

Community schools are an effective reform strategy because they pay concurrent and equal attention to teaching and learning. They work to implement a rigorous and coherent core instructional program, to enrich and extend students' learning opportunities in the nonschool hours, and to remove barriers to student success through increased access to medical, dental, mental health, and social services.

Community schools across the country are getting better and more consistent results than traditional schools because they engage parents as partners in their children's education—welcoming parents, helping them develop strategies for supporting their own children's education, and recruiting community partners with skills in reaching and assisting families on an ongoing basis and in stabilizing them during times of crisis.

The U.S. Secretary of Education recognizes the considerable merit of the community schools strategy, based on his seven-year tenure as chief executive officer of the Chicago public schools. For example, at an October 2009 national community schools conference sponsored by the Children's Aid Society, Arne Duncan noted that "making every school a community school . . . that's got to be our collective vision. Not just isolated islands of extended time, but really the norm for every single student." Duncan went on to observe:

> And if we go across the country—rich, poor, white, Latino communities—we have schools, and in every school we have classrooms, there is a computer lab, there are libraries, gyms, some have pools. And in far too many places, the community does not have access to that. But those schools don't belong to me, they don't belong to the principal, they don't all belong to the board, they don't belong to the union. They belong to the community. And we have to think about using these great assets to change the life chances of our children . . . So the more our schools become community centers—not just open for children but their older brothers and sisters, their families, GED classes, ESL classes, whatever it might be, the more families are engaged, the more schools become the heart of family life—the better our students are going to do.

What would it take to translate this vision—shared by so many practitioners, researchers, funders, advocates, and even with the nation's top education official—into a reality for all schools?

First, it would take a huge paradigm shift, a "vision implant" of sorts. Our society would have to come up with innovative twenty-first-century answers to such central questions as Who owns the public schools? Who bears accountability for student success? What price does our society pay for the glaring achievement gap that now exists between more and less affluent children?

Second, it would take much greater alignment between and among the many players whose work contributes to student success. What might we be able to accomplish if we were able to align city and county services and public and private funding from all sources around student success? What if federal policy supported that alignment? What if the several partners shared accountability for results and agreed to measure the collective impact of their efforts?

Here are several promising approaches and ideas that could, if implemented widely, help achieve Arne Duncan's stated vision of *every school a community school*:

Federal Policy

If there is one thing we have learned from reform efforts of the past decade, it is that federal education policy can have a tremendous influence on local education practice. The effects of the 2002 No Child Left Behind legislation have been felt in every U.S. city and town, despite our country's collective consciousness about and commitment to local control of its public schools. The pending reauthorization of the Elementary and Secondary Education Act (the major federal education legislation, of which No Child Left Behind is the current iteration) holds great potential for moving the needle toward widespread implementation of community schools.

This great potential has led the Coalition for Community Schools to make ESEA reauthorization its major policy focus over the past two years. The Coalition's most recent policy brief on this topic makes the following recommendations to the U.S. Congress:

- Integrate community schools into the ESEA statute as an allowable school intervention model;
- Require comprehensive accountability frameworks (that include but go beyond standardized tests as a measure of school and student success);
- Provide incentives for results-driven public/private partnerships;
- Enable community-school coordination;
- Promote family and youth engagement;
- Ensure effective professional development;
- Support capacity building (around comprehensive, integrated approaches to school reform);

TOURO COLLEGE LIBRARY

• Align and coordinate the Department of Education and other federal agency resources.

The timetable for reauthorization of ESEA is uncertain, which has led the U.S. Department of Education to allow states to request waivers to many of the mandates and provisions in No Child Left Behind. However, given the centrality of ESEA to the work of expanding and supporting community schools, the coalition and its 170 partners (including the authors of this book) will continue to advocate for inclusion of the specific recommendations outlined above and detailed in the coalition's policy brief (Coalition for Community Schools, 2011).

State Policy

If state policy were aligned with the kind of supportive federal policy outlined above, states would take a more comprehensive, holistic view of student development and success; they would allocate resources to expansion of community schools through state-level discretionary grants programs (similar to the Healthy Start state legislation and funding in California); they would align their state 21st Century Community Learning Centers and Child Care Development Block Grant allocations from the federal government with a community schools approach; and they would pass and enforce policies that support a comprehensive and integrated approach to education (similar to the New York state guidelines on social and emotional learning that were recently passed by the New York State Board of Regents).

County Policy

Many parts of the United States have vibrant county governments with control of substantial resources that could be used to support the implementation and expansion of community schools. Robust examples of policy frameworks and funding allocations that support community schools exist in such places as Multnomah County (Oregon) and Kent County (Michigan). In both of these (and other) cases, the county governments are working in partnership with municipal governments to share and align their human and financial resources, using schools as services hubs and community centers. As a result of policy shifts, county human service and health and mental health workers may be redeployed from central offices to schools, providing students and families much easier access to needed supports and services.

YOUNG COLLEGE LIBRARY

City/District Policy

Several districts, including Cincinnati and Hartford, have passed explicit policies stating that they welcome partnerships with community resources that are aligned with their student success goals. The Cincinnati policy begins with a statement that the Cincinnati public schools belong to the people of Cincinnati—an observation that mirrors the statements of the U.S. Secretary of Education cited earlier (and that flies in the face of much educational practice).

Other Alignment Strategies

If community schools are truly seen as "a strategy for organizing the resources of the community around student success," then they provide a platform for aligning the funding and leadership of many other partners—United Ways, community foundations, higher education, teachers' unions, local human service councils, the faith community, businesses, adult service clubs, and others. All of these community resources are partners in community schools around the country, and many of them (including the National Education Association and the American Federation of Teachers) are active members of the Coalition for Community Schools.

Schools like Thomas Edison Elementary School represent both an "existence proof" and an inspiration in the noisy world of school reform. They stand as a testament to the good will of community partners that have come together to welcome newcomers, to share their resources, to hold one another accountable for positive results, and to work on behalf of the community's common good. They exemplify the translation of current research into action. And, in the words of U.S. Congressman Steny Hoyer (National Center for Community Schools, 2011), a leading champion of community schools, they just "make good sense."

Chapter Seven

A Toolkit of Resources, Ideas, and Inspirations

FROM THE DIRECTOR OF THE NATIONAL CENTER FOR COMMUNITY SCHOOLS: MY FIRST VISIT TO A COMMUNITY SCHOOL

I still remember my first visit to a community school. I was working as the program director at the DeWitt Wallace-Reader's Digest Fund, where our grant-making team was beginning to get interested in the community schools strategy after having read Joy Dryfoos's groundbreaking 1994 book on full-service schools. It was probably 1996.

I walked into Intermediate School 218 in the New York City neighborhood of Washington Heights, a low-income area that served as the American port of entry for Dominican immigrants. I remember standing in the foyer of the school and immediately observing two things: the students looked happy, and there were a lot of adults, more than I was used to seeing in traditional schools. And I thought to myself: "I wonder what is happening here, and I wonder how we can make it happen in more places."

This recollection brings us back to our purpose in helping readers successfully launch their own community school initiatives. This chapter is thus intended to provide a number of resources and ideas that we have found useful from our own work experiences and ones that we hope will serve to inform and inspire the work of others. These resources will ultimately minimize and even help avoid some of the pitfalls we have encountered over the years.

The chapter is divided into three sections, with the first devoted to initiating the community school strategy, the second to assessing progress and continuing implementation, and the third directed to enhancing one's general knowledge of related resources.

INITIATING THE COMMUNITY SCHOOL STRATEGY

An important early step in transforming a traditional school into a community school involves conducting a needs assessment—a systematic process used to understand and create a profile of the school. Without a current and comprehensive needs assessment, a school is unlikely to maximize the potential of the community schools strategy—a strategy designed to organize school and community resources around student success.

The purpose of the needs assessment is *not* to rigorously or scientifically evaluate the impact of individual programs or curricula but, instead, to gather a wide range of information that will inform and drive decisions about the community school's programming and information. This process often involves three steps: (1) reviewing data from multiple sources; (2) conducting an inventory of the school's current supports and services, including those provided by the school (such as the school nurse and school social worker) and those provided by external partners; and (3) conducting a gap analysis that identifies unmet needs of students and families.

In the first step of the process, the planning team gathers, analyzes, and organizes data from multiple sources, including the school, district, and neighborhood. Typically, planners review student achievement and attendance data, school suspension rates, after-school attendance, community health statistics, and school and community safety indicators. These kinds of data are generally available quite readily. Other relevant data, such as rates of chronic absence in a particular school, may require additional manipulation and the synthesis of data from multiple sources.

Based on this initial data review, planners often continue the needs assessment process by gathering additional information through focus groups, interviews, and/or surveys in order to ascertain the view of key stakeholders, including teachers, parents, and students. Although not included in this book, the National Center for Community Schools has developed a detailed Needs Assessment Toolkit that can help in this process. We have included one of the tools from this toolkit, *Needs Assessment Report Outline* (textbox 7.1) to assist in planning work.

The second step involves conducting a resource inventory at the school, which identifies current supports and services available to students and families. This inventory should be comprehensive in scope, and should include supports and services provided by the school as well as those provided by partners. Readers are free to use and adapt table 7.1 (Resource Inventory) to aid in this part of the planning process.

The third step is to create a Need Gap Analysis Worksheet (see table 7.2), based on the review of current information about the school. This worksheet

Textbox 7.1. Needs Assessment Report Outline

I. Introduction and Background
This section describes the purpose of the needs assessment and the specific questions and issues the assessment was designed to explore. Background information on the community school initiative should also be included here briefly.

II. Methods
This section describes all of the methods used to collect the data and information presented in the report as well as the key participants (or participant types) involved in the processes.

a. Data Collection
Brief description of each data collection method used:

- Archival Data Review—list all data sources that were consulted
- Surveys—include a description of the groups that received and submitted surveys, including how representative each sample was of their larger population
- Focus Group—include a description of the number and types of groups that participated
- Interviews—include a description of the individuals that were interviewed

b. Strengths and Limitations
Description of the main strengths of the process (for example, a large number of archival data sources were available), as well as any considerations the audience should be aware of as they read and interpret the key findings (i.e., poor participant response rates on parent surveys).

c. Key Participants
List of the primary participants who administered the process, including those who collected the data and the members of the committee who analyzed and interpreted the information presented in the report.

III. Key Findings
This section summarizes the analyses and findings from the process. A bulleted list is easier to read and act on over a lengthy narrative.

IV. Recommendations
This section describes the implications from the data and suggests next steps for your community school.

V. Appendices
Included in this section should be the data collection instruments used, such as the survey and focus group questions, and the schedule of activities that contributed to the process.
Source: National Center for Community Schools, *Building Community Schools: A Guide for Action*, 2011

outlines the five developmental domains and allows teams to plan how the needs of the "whole child" will be addressed in the community school. It should be noted that the National Center for Community Schools has chosen the terms *cognitive* and *moral* in lieu of the terms *intellectual* and *ethical* used throughout this book. Readers should use the language most appropriate to their school settings.

Once this initial planning has been conducted, it is likely that partners will be recruited who can help fill in the gaps that have been identified. We have found it useful to craft Memoranda of Understanding (MOU) with all external partners. An MOU represents a contract clearly articulating the detailed elements of the partner relationship, inclusive of all roles, responsibilities, and methods of funding. Table 7.3 provides a template of an MOU agreement with corresponding items that will require further discussion and written descriptions related to each by all involved in partnership prior to the implementation of any program or service.

THE PRINCIPAL'S PERSPECTIVE: MORE THAN A "HANDSHAKE," THE MOU AS AN ESSENTIAL INGREDIENT TO SUCCESSFUL PARTNERSHIP WITHIN A COMMUNITY SCHOOL

Early in Edison's evolution as a community school, several of our partnerships were literally formed "by a handshake"; however, we quickly learned, and sometimes the hard way, that the MOU is essential to spelling out the details of a formal relationship. If left unattended, such details have the potential to deter both the community school vision and those of its partners.

It's also worth noting that funding streams and program needs in community schools with demonstrated longevity often change over time.

At Edison, for example, a single position in a given year could be paid for through one or more funding sources including Title I, Title III, the general fund, and special grants (local, state or federal), with modifications of job descriptions put into place to comply with any new funding guidelines and restrictions. For this reason, similar to the school's Strategic Action Plan, the MOU document should be reviewed and revised annually with appropriate partner approvals whenever such changes are necessary.

As part of the initial work of transforming a traditional school into a community school, the hiring of a community school director (or site coordinator) is strongly recommended. As stated earlier in this book, this person may work for a lead agency or directly for the school or district. In Edison's case, the director was employed, through grant funding, directly by the school district. In many other initiatives, the community school director is employed by and reports to the lead agency. However, in both cases, the director's role is to partner with the school's principal, to develop external partnerships that respond to the assessment of student and family needs, and to integrate those partnerships (whether they are provided by the lead agency or other partners) with the school's core instructional program. Textbox 7.2 provides a sample job description for this role.

ASSESSING PROGRESS
AND CONTINUING IMPLEMENTATION

Over the past twenty years of community schools implementation across the country, practitioners have learned that there are typical stages of development as they work to transform their traditional school into a community school. The National Center for Community Schools began to document this process, which has resulted in a well-accepted Stages of Development Tool that has guided work across the field for more than a decade. This tool (figure 7.1) can serve as a road map that indicates both ultimate destinations (Excelling stage) and landmarks along the way.

The Stages of Development Tool is extremely useful because it defines the nature and scope of organizational competencies or "capacities" that are essential to community schools. This tool is helpful to community schools at various stages of implementation, keeping leadership teams focused on the school's level of functioning related to critical principles and practices in community schools.

Table 7.1. Resource Inventory

Programs Provided Agency/Type of Program	Academic skills for youth (e.g., tutoring, homework help)	Enrichment (e.g., photography, chess, etc.)	Recreation for youth (e.g., sports)	Early childhood (e.g., childcare, parenting classes)	Parent/Family Resource Center	Community building (e.g., family /community empowerment)	Adult education classes (e.g., GED, ESL)
			# Youth Served and (# Families/Adults Served)				

Services Provided	Health Services			Mental Health Services Substance/ Alcohol Abuse Counseling	General Social Services (e.g., access to health insurance, immigration, food pantry, etc.)
Agency/Type of Service	Medical	Vision	Dental services (Ortho, etc.)		
# Youth Served and (# Families/Adults Served)					

Source: National Center for Community Schools, *Building Community Schools: A Guide for Action*, 2011

Table 7.2. Need Gap Analysis Worksheet

Develop-mental domain	List programs and services provided for each domain	Who's not being served? Whose needs are not being met? ID gaps.	Who has the capacity to meet the unmet needs?	What can be done to address the gaps?
Physical				
Cognitive				
Emotional				
Social				
Moral				

Source: National Center for Community Schools, *Building Community Schools: A Guide for Action*, 2011

Table 7.3. MOU Development Template

Period of Agreement: _____
(Identify names of partner agency, school district, and school) agree to assume and perform the following roles and responsibilities in the administration of the (identify program).

MOU Agreement Items	Partner Organization	School	Joint: Partner & School	District	Joint: Organization & District
Allocation of building space(s) and custodial maintenance					
Construction needs					
Services offered (and exclusions)					
Scheduling and hours of operation					
Staffing (including job descriptions/qualifications, hiring/evaluating/terminating procedures, and the payment of applicable salaries and benefits)					
Materials, supplies, and equipment					
Transportation (if applicable)					
Fees (if applicable)					
Liabilities and insurance					
Systems for communication and reporting across and within organizations					
Governance and advisory structures					
Protocols for emergencies					
Systems for resolving conflict					
Record keeping and clerical support					
Coordination of recruitment/ referrals, enrollment, and registration for participants					
Establishment and evaluation of performance objectives, aligned with school and program goals					
Termination and modification of agreement procedures					

Agreed on this date, _____ by,
Partner_____
District_____
School Principal_____

Textbox 7.2. The Role of a Community School Director (CSD) or Coordinator

Preferred Qualifications: Master's Degree in Social Work, Education, or a Related Field Administrative Experience

Bilingual Ability in English and the High Incidence Community Language

The Community School Director may be the lead agency's on-site representative who serves as liaison and partner with the principal or may work directly for the school district under the supervision of the principal and/or district personnel. The roles and responsibilities of the CSD are as follows:

- Coleads the community school (with the principal)—Together, they help craft the vision and engage and excite others about it, ensure that programming is supporting this vision and guides the general direction of the partnerships. The CSD serves as the lead for community school programs and ensures their functioning.
- Manages programs—Monitors program quality, appropriateness, responsiveness, and timeliness; ensures alignment of day and afternoon programs; develops procedures and policies as needed; ensures that programming promotes developmentally appropriate skills and supports all developmental domains; ensures programming is culturally appropriate and responsive to the populations served.
- Educates—Provides information on the partnership, educates on the nature and scope of the partnership, and helps others to understand their role in it.
- Brokers and tends relationships to strengthen the partnership and what it offers to the school and families.
- Develops and enhances parental involvement in the schools through the use of dedicated activities and the resources of the community school and its partners.
- Engages the community by attending or convening activities that involve the community.
- Oversees or leads communication and public education about the community school.

- Develops strong partnership with the principal through joint planning, ongoing communication, and problem solving and by providing technical assistance as needed.
- Engages the community in the community school's vision by creating opportunities for involvement with the school, helping the school maintain a "swinging door" that brings the community into the school to participate and assist, and reaching out to the community to contribute to its betterment.
- Participates actively in schoolwide planning and governance teams.
- Assures that the hours of operation and the supervision in the school fulfill the basic principles of community schools: extending the school day, week, and year for children and families.
- In collaboration with community school partners and/or lead agency, prepares and monitors site budget(s).

For Community School Directors serving under a lead agency and acting as its on-site representative:

- Organizational representative—Represents his/her organizational interest and priorities in the partnership; ensures that the organizational competencies are used and add value to the school; educates others in the organization about the partnership, and, as appropriate, advocates for the partnership needs within the organization.

Source: National Center for Community Schools, *Building Community Schools: A Guide for Action*, 2011

However, community schools are not "transformed" overnight and often demonstrate movement that is not always parallel in all areas. A change in conditions or events, for example, may sometimes dictate movement backward along the continuum of developmental stages, but need not result in stagnation. Persistence and patience should therefore be exercised and this valuable tool for continued growth in implementation can be used to help keep schools moving forward.

Figure 7.1. Stages of Development

Over fifteen years of practice, both managing and training in the development of community schools, the National Center for Community Schools has promoted the use of "Stages of Development" to help practitioners and policymakers understand where they are on the continuum of community schools and what they need to do to move forward. We believe that each initiative and each site must develop a set of four capacities:

- Comprehensiveness
- Collaboration
- Coherence
- Commitment

This document summarizes the features of community schools at four stages:

- Exploring
- Emerging
- Maturing
- Excelling

There is a considerable amount of information contained under these four capacities. For most effective use, focus either on one set of practices across all four stages OR focus on one stage of development and examine the practices listed. Note throughout that a site or an initiative can easily be at one stage in one practice and in quite a different stage for another, indicating areas of focus for your work.

Capacity: Comprehensiveness

Principles and Practices	Stage 1: Exploring	Stage 2: Emerging	Stage 3: Maturing	Stage 4: Excelling
Community schools build their vision from a comprehensive understanding of the developmental needs of children and youth and seek to address the major developmental domains (cognitive, social, emotional, physical, moral) in ways that promote student success.	*Characterized by recognition that children and families have multiple needs that impact school climate and inhibit learning, and that schools cannot address them alone. Focus on how to get services and programs for children and families, both nonacademic and academic enrichment.*	*Characterized by initial steps toward building relationship with a lead partner and other willing providers. School open extended hours for partners to provide services, as well as inviting programming and support services during the school day.*	*Characterized by opening school to multiple partner services and programs that respond to identified needs of students, school, families, and community and that improve the overall conditions for learning.*	*Characterized by a shift in role of schools as hubs of opportunity and civic engagement for students, families, and neighborhoods residents. System in place for ongoing comprehensiveness in response to need and demand.*

Whole Child Perspective Underlying approach recognizes that school success results from positive development in all the major domains, not just cognitive. Social-emotional learning understood to contribute to and support academic achievement. CS approach recognizes the importance of the family, school, and community as context for student development.	Focus on shared learning of high-quality principles and approaches: • academic enhancement • child and youth development • parent involvement and family strengthening • community development	Complementary programs target identified needs: • initial programs/services may be added by opportunity • program resource development prioritized by need • referrals to programs identified by need • family and community need considered	Major areas of developmental concern are being addressed by programming and/or linkages: • academic support and enhancement • cultural enrichment/skill development • physical and mental health • family social services, adult education • early childhood • community safety and development	Academic, social, health, and developmental needs are systematically being addressed: • Opportunities to progress along continuum of programming • Developmental opportunities fuel academic success • Developmental opportunities fuel improved related outcomes

Responsiveness to Need
Systematic assessment of needs—of each target population, school climate, and community context—grounds decisions about resource allocation and partnership recruitment. Existing resources are well understood and evaluated for alignment with results framework of the community school.
	Initial needs assessment and mapping of existing resources in school and in community:
	• leadership "brainstorming"
	• discussions with stakeholder groups
	• study of existing community and school data
		In-depth, ongoing needs assessment and resource mapping:
		• Surveys/focus groups with all stakeholder groups:
		  • parents
		  • school staff
		  • students
		  • community residents
		  • partners
		• Systems put in place to monitor school and community data
			Program utilization is linked to need and monitored for outcomes:
			• needs assessment is institutionalized as ongoing process; regular channels exist for input and feedback
			• appropriate students/families linked to needed services and programs by site coordinator and school staff
			• enrichment activities complement school-day program
			• school facilities offer numerous opportunities in out-of-school time
				Partner-provided and school-provided programs jointly meet district and community goals:
				• needs assessment addresses individual need, population needs, and community needs
				• assets/resources of community are fully integrated to target challenges
				• new challenges regularly brought to CS for coordinated responses

Figure 7.1. *(Continued)*

Principles and Practices	Stage 1: Exploring	Stage 2: Emerging	Stage 3: Maturing	Stage 4: Excelling

High-Quality Programs and Services The array of activities and services offered is designed to augment, enrich, and increase the capacity of each target group. Scarce resources are directed at identified needs and targeted to appropriate populations in order to achieve agreed priority results.	Some partner programs and services may already exist in school. Partners and schools begin to explore how to improve:
	• access to services
	• coordination
	• integration
	• targeting to identified needs and results
	• quality assurance
		Developmentally appropriate programs added as resourced:
		• resource development for needed programs and services
		• attention paid to quality programming:
		  • youth development
		  • family strengthening
		  • community empowerment
		• use needs data and best practices
			Principles of youth development, family strengthening, and community development underpin program content:
			• core competencies of partner agencies are fully used
			• school and partner programs use common philosophical approaches
			• programs and services are perceived as desirable, fun, responsive by students, families, and neighbors
				School is seen as a vibrant, busy center for activities desired by its community, as well as locus of effective service delivery and active civic engagement in education:
				• schools are partners of choice for new programs and opportunities
				• community has confidence in school as access point for responsiveness
				• school seen as purveyor of excitement, opportunity, and hope

Capacity: Collaboration

Principles and Practices	Stage 1: Exploring	Stage 2: Emerging	Stage 3: Maturing	Stage 4: Excelling
In community schools, multiple partners develop the trusting relationships and the capacity to work smoothly together with authentically shared leadership and mutual accountability for shared results.	*Characterized by interest in CS strategy as way to engage others in removing barriers and improving conditions for learning. Open to sharing leadership. Interested in increasing parental and community engagement.*	*Characterized by increased efforts to engage parents and community in planning, implementation, and oversight of academic and nonacademic programs. Beginning to involve partners and parents in decision making.*	*Characterized by the regular involvement and leadership of wide range of stakeholders. Transparent agreements and mutual accountability underpin the ongoing development of partnerships.*	*Characterized by permanent engagement across community, collaborative mode of community and program development, and policymaking.*
Community Engagement Civic engagement in schools will increase their success. Community acts as advocate, supporter, partner, service user, and guardian that holds schools accountable for student success.	Recognition of the connection between success of school and thriving community: • engagement of community leadership in efforts to improve conditions for students • interest in school as center of community • importance of community conditions recognized (e.g., safety, environment, housing) • public interest in increasing civic engagement in education	Clear communication and engagement of community in planning and implementation: • public education about CS strategy • may establish agreements with community residents, businesses, organizations to provide services to students and families • community representation on all governing and coordinating bodies	CS is responsive to needs of the community and generates regular community events and programs: • increased visibility, public celebrations • services directed at community needs, accessible in school/nonschool hours • community represented in leadership • community-based learning opportunities • parents and youth encouraged to become community leaders	Community regularly uses schools as venues for problem-solving, cultural celebration, development, engagement: • "swinging door" access for community members and organizations as providers of and participants in school-based opportunities • joint planning and accountability with community • community members rally as advocates for CS strategy

Principles and Practices	Stage 1: Exploring	Stage 2: Emerging	Stage 3: Maturing	Stage 4: Excelling
Partnerships Schools and one or more organizations with a shared vision and resources come together to serve students, their families, and the community. Agreements are structured to ensure clarity of roles and shared accountability.	Openness to agencies and organizations with services and programs essential to student success: • study of models of partnership • willingness to share leadership, accountability	Formal agreement with lead partner shifts some responsibilities to partner staff: • principal begins sharing management of building, activities, and scheduling • joint decision making in agreed areas of work	Lead partners serve as lead point-of-contact for all school partnerships: • agreements in place for all providers • monitoring and accountability • shared responsibility of partners and school staff for success of students • shared philosophies of youth development & family strengthening	Seamless coordination among permanent and mobile partners: • Systems allow for occasional and long-term partnerships to evolve, with monitoring and accountability assured
Governance Structures and processes are created through which shared leadership is institutionalized and decisions are made for CS. A coordinating body and leadership team at the school level must bring all partners into regular and active communication, giving voice to all perspectives. At the initiative level, a resource coordination/policy development body is important. Midlevel management collaboration may also require institutionalization.	Interest in sharing leadership and responsibility for success of students: • principal and district leaders retain sole responsibility for school facilities and programs • existing school leadership teams and structures are in place • informal networks may also be at work to support school and students	Formal governance structures, agreements built around shared vision and objectives: • selection of lead partner and agreement on roles • decision-making and communication processes developed among school, lead partner, and providers • development of coordinating body with representative stakeholders • memoranda of understanding (MOU) or letters of agreement (LOA) concluded District and municipal policy leadership develop governance structures as well.	Governance bodies effectively institutionalized within schools: • leadership committees include needed representation of relevant stakeholder groups • mission and strategies integrated with school improvement plan • CS coordinating bodies enhance existing school committees Vertical communication among levels of governance (school site, district, regional, etc.) is responsive, transparent, and effective.	School-site and communitywide governance in place and functioning as part of public and private networks: • management issues efficiently responded to • flow of ideas and concerns is smooth, up and down the governance chain • linkages to political systems ensure effectiveness and relevance

Capacity: Coherence

Principles and Practices In community schools, a shared vision drives the alignment of community resources toward student success. Effective management structures, communications, and logistics are institutionalized in support of the whole child, family, and community.	**Stage 1: Exploring** *Characterized by recognition that effective management of needed programs and services exceeds capacity of existing staffing and structures. Recognized need for program integration. Planning process engages all stakeholders.*	**Stage 2: Emerging** *Characterized by efforts to develop effective coordination and system of monitoring and accountability for programs and services. Development of new resources for staffing, communication patterns, management.*	**Stage 3: Maturing** *Characterized by the integration of CS structure/processes/programs into "normal" operations of schools. Site coordinator role is clearly understood, and leadership is reliably shared. Effective, consistent management is a hallmark of this stage.*	**Stage 4: Excelling** *Characterized by policy shifts that make CS a permanent approach to school reform, service delivery, community-based education, and civic engagement.*
Integration The process of aligning diverse and separate programs and activities into a coherent, congruent whole around an agreed set of results. Participation of CS leadership in school's regular teams and regular communication between partners and educators are key features of well-integrated initiatives.	Interest in moving toward more comprehensive, integrated system: • programs and services are not integrated with the school's academic program • programs and services not highly integrated with one another • limited integration may exist through district-mandated structures	Extended-day programming complements content of school-day curriculum: • initial efforts to align enrichment program with state and district standards • initial efforts to open communication between staff of school and program partners • develop coordinating body for regular communication among various providers	Extended-day programming developed in concert with school staff and addresses school learning priorities, as well as school climate: • program referrals from established Pupil (Student) Support Teams • content developed in collaboration with school staff	Joint development of academic and extended-day programs, with curriculum enhancement provided by partners and teachers together: • partners' cost-sharing contributes to optimal programming • shared delivery of content • connection to community-based learning • shared responsibility for success

Figure 7.1. *(Continued)*

Principles and Practices	Stage 1: Exploring	Stage 2: Emerging	Stage 3: Maturing	Stage 4: Excelling
Management and Staffing Paid and volunteer personnel are used to accomplish the tasks and activities of the CS. Key staff positions include Community School Director/Site Coordinator and Parent Coordinator/Liaison. Regular consultation between leadership and key school administrators is critical. Smooth logistical and communication strategies in place.	Desire for principal's primary role to be instructional leader: • Principal remains sole manager of all activities in building • No formal budget exists for program and coordination staffing • Volunteers may play roles in management but with little coordination or planning	Site Coordinator (title varies) assuming responsibility for agreed set of responsibilities: • budget established for coordination functions • additional roles may be played by staff or volunteers (parent coordinator, etc.) • program staff provided per grant sources	Well-trained program staff, coordinated by CS director, supported by school and community volunteers, provide high-quality, well-used programming: • consistent practices across providers • enrollment, disciplinary, and termination policies aligned • leadership opportunities for program graduates, parents • new staff acculturated to collaboration	Programs become part of enhancement of employment, volunteerism, and leadership development for community: • staff promoted to become leaders in new CS sites, coach new staff • CS programs enhance and improve quality of academic instruction • Common standards of quality enhance wide range of school- and community-based programs
Family Engagement The underlying philosophy and daily practice reflecting the belief that parents/caregivers are key to student success, and must be included in school life at all levels.	Awareness of impact of parental involvement on academic success: • PTA/PTO, existing school policies, or no functioning formal structures; some natural leadership • study of successful family engagement strategies • informal parent groupings around natural commonalities	Energized focus on family engagement as advocates, volunteers, partners in education: • parents involved in all levels of planning, needs/assets assessment, governance bodies • scheduled parent activities • active parent leadership bodies • reliable communication between CS and parents • parent space being developed in school	Parents present in wide range of supportive roles for entire community school: • effective as decision makers in governance structures of school • using dedicated parent space with access to information, technology, etc. • leadership development and opportunities for parents, including as volunteers and staff • connected at home to learning process	Parents both take advantage of and generate/provide elements of programming and are fully empowered as leaders: • provide leadership development for other parents • trusted partners for school and provider organizations, as well as at levels of governance • serve as advocates and spokespeople for CS in policy-making arenas

Capacity: Commitment

Principles and Practices
Actions and communications reflect intention to remain partners for the long term, independent of any particular grants or initial funding stream or political scenario.

Sustainability Planning
Key partners act in such a way as to sustain the initiative through time and across changing political realities. Includes:
- shared vision
- broad support of community/leaders
- agreed set of results
- strategic financing: public/private funds

Stage 1: Exploring
Characterized by an interest in building the CS for the long term, with policy changes, systems, resources, and engagement geared toward permanency.

Conversations begin with wide range of stakeholders:
- results framework developed in collaborative process
- policy leaders involved in planning, collaborative structures
- financing options are investigated, including grants, public funds, in-kind services

Stage 2: Emerging
Characterized by systematic, multiyear efforts to collect data, build focus on results, seek resources, and build support.

Sustainability activities are regular work of staff and governance bodies:
- resource development is multiyear
- policy changes to align existing public funding integrate with broader public goals
- networking within initiatives at perhaps systemic level
- garner commitments from policymakers

Stage 3: Maturing
Characterized by growing realization that CS can provide coordination and targeting for numerous child/family/community goals. Policy and funding decisions begin to reflect site successes.

Results in CS sites are connected with broader goals and agendas, providing rationale for increased support:
- key policymakers taking ownership, backed by community demand
- collaborative, strategic proposal writing
- advocacy for alignment of existing funds
- connections to related initiatives
- CS strategy enters political discourse

Stage 4: Excelling
Characterized by permanent political commitment, designated funding, private and community support, alignment of related initiatives, using CS as coordinating strategy.

CS strategy seen as integral to regional service delivery and to the new definitions of "school" and "community":
- schools seen as locus of family strengthening, access to resources
- schools seen as centers of community development
- public and private funding aligned

Figure 7.1. *(Continued)*

	Stage 1: Exploring	Stage 2: Emerging	Stage 3: Maturing	Stage 4: Excelling
Principles and Practices Evaluation Assessment of the process & impact of programs & partnership on the target population. Includes the systematic collection, analysis, and use of data in programs.	Understanding of need to document positive impact of CS activities: • informal observations • some may have concern for costs of evaluation • identification of program objectives • resource development for formal evaluation	Systematic collection of relevant data tied to results: • closely analyze process data (utilization, satisfaction, etc.) for use in quality improvement • using preliminary data, demonstrate correlation between need and utilization • generate baselines for outcome research	Comprehensive evaluation underway and beginning to show outputs, outcomes: • meaningful data demonstrate improvements in key indicators (e.g., attendance, safety) • commitment to full funding for multiyear evaluation • Early results broadly communicated to generate future commitments	Ongoing evaluation demonstrates effectiveness and areas for improvement: • continuous looping of information informs policymaking and capacity building • planning informed by past successes and shortcomings • commitment to evaluation sustained
Marketing and Communications A developed capacity to communicate the impact and the value of the community school on academic achievement, child and youth development, family and community well-being; and to convey confidence in the management systems that undergird these efforts.	Plan development is shared with stakeholders: • can experience concern over new approach and/or cynicism about past efforts • ways in which different stakeholders can participate and benefit are communicated • leaders strive for maximum transparency	Regular communication vehicles selected and implemented: • newsletters, websites, blogs, chat rooms, hotlines, calendars, etc., enable free flow of communication among multiple stakeholders • regular reporting from leadership/governance bodies to all stakeholders of policy development	Communication practices effectively link all stakeholders and engage them in planning, implementation, and utilization: • keep pace with times • use appropriate technologies, maintaining sensitivity to various communication pathways of stakeholders • media used to publicize CS activities	Information flows in multiple directions through multiple pathways: • partners integrate CS into internal and external communications • public media regularly transmit information about CS • successes are regularly publicized; communications and media mobilize public will to sustain CS

Capacity Building Creating infrastructure to build capacity of all stakeholders and among sites within initiative.	Begin to understand that there is a body of knowledge from both research and practice that can guide CS implementation: • leadership development • understanding four capacities, associated practices, and activities • developing skills at all levels	Establish training and networking opportunities at all levels: • develop intermediary with capacity-building skills • consistent message about centrality of capacity building in CS systems • create developmental ethic at all levels	Ongoing training/ networking at all levels of initiative: program, site coordination, management, and governance: • training and coaching functions are budgeted and regularly scheduled • accountable for skill/ knowledge development • connection to national movement	Initiative perpetuates excellence as it grows, provides opportunities for leaders to train and coach others: • develops own procedures and best practices as teaching tools • serves as regional site for expanded learning

Source: National Center for Community Schools, *Building Community Schools: A Guide for Action,* 2011

Another central issue in schools—one that community schools pay particular attention to—is school climate. Research shows that a positive school climate is a key ingredient of effective schools. The National Center for Community Schools developed two resources to help schools assess their current climate (figure 7.2) and develop an action plan for its improvement (figure 7.3).

Readers are again reminded that the Center has used the terms *cognitive* and *moral* in their publications; however, as authors, we have used the terms *intellectual* and *ethical* interchangeably for these terms. This choice was made based on Edison's early involvement with the Child Development Project and the school's long-standing commitment to the Eleven Principles of Effective Character Education (Character Education Partnership, 2010).

The Center's School Climate Self-Assessment and Action Planning tools are best used by a group of stakeholders rather than one individual. Students should be included as key informants in helping to assess school climate, along with teachers, administrators, partners, and parents. Experience has taught us that this type of data gathering works well in meeting formats that allow for a representative group of stakeholders to first reflect upon the tool individually and then to follow up with a group discussion since each may not be totally familiar with all of the programs, practices, and services in operation related to each of the five elements of climate. This tool could than be completed as a group.

The construction of these tools takes into account of the "whole child," with concerted attention to the physical, social, emotional, intellectual, and ethical aspects of human development and how each of these domains is supported by the school's environment. In addition to their specific value in helping to assess and improve school climate, these tools can reiterate the importance for all stakeholders of keeping the whole child at the center of their collective attention at all times.

Figure 7.2. Community School Climate Self-Assessment Tool

This instrument is organized under the five elements of climate in a community school. For each element, standards of practice—or "indicators"—are listed to provide you with clear guidelines of what contributes to a positive climate in a community school. Use the rating system described below to assess the quality of your community school's climate. Add comments as necessary.

Rating System

4 Excellent/Exceeds Standard
3 Satisfactory/Meets Standard
2 Some Progress Made/Approaching Standard
1 Must Address and Improve/Standard Not Met

I. Physical Environment

An environment that is safe, welcoming, and conducive to learning	Rating				Comments
Indicators:	1	2	3	4	
1.	Space (e.g., library, media center) is shared and accessible to everyone.				
2.	Staff and students are—and feel—safe everywhere on school property.				
3.	Classrooms and grounds are clean and well maintained.				
4.	School equipment is maintained, up-to-date, and available to students, families, or community.				
5.	Class size and ratio of students to teacher are conducive to learning.				
6.	School facilities allow for cocurricular activities.				
7.	Noise level is appropriate for learning and activities being conducted.				
8.	Areas for instruction and activities are appropriate for those uses.				

Figure 7.2. *(Continued)*

		1	2	3	4	Comments
9.	School and classrooms are visible and inviting (e.g., print-rich displays and work created by students and families).					
10.	School and partner staff members have sufficient books and supplies to maximize participation of all students.					
11.	Clear rules and norms regarding safety and expected behavior are visually displayed throughout the school.					

II. Social Environment

An environment that promotes communication, interactions, and relationship building		Rating				Comments
Indicators:		1	2	3	4	
1.	Open, honest, and active communication occurs (teachers and students, teachers and parents, school and community, etc.).					
2.	Teachers/staff are collegial. They support and work collaboratively around the achievement and success of the students.					
3.	Student groupings are diverse.					
4.	Parents and teachers/staff are partners in the educational process.					
5.	Decisions are made on-site, with the participation of teachers/staff.					
6.	School faculty and staff are open to suggestions (from students, families, community). All stakeholders have opportunities to participate in decision making.					
7.	Families are encouraged to participate and develop relationships with the faculty and staff as well as with other families.					

			Rating				
8.	There are extracurricular opportunities that emphasize group work and improve ties between students.						
9.	Parents/families and community members get involved in the planning and organization of school functions.						
10.	Networks of support exist (peer mentors, clubs, family resource centers).						

III. Affective/Emotional Environment

An environment that promotes a sense of belonging and self-esteem		Rating				Comments
Indicators:		1	2	3	4	
1.	Interactions between teachers/staff and students are caring, responsive, supportive, and respectful (also administration to staff, peer-to-peer, staff to families, etc.).					
2.	Students trust teachers and staff.					
3.	Morale is high among teachers and staff.					
4.	Staff, students, and families demonstrate school pride.					
5.	The school values diversity and is welcoming to all cultures.					
6.	Teachers/staff, students, and families are respected and valued.					
7.	Teachers/staff and students and families feel that they are contributing to the success of the school.					
8.	The school is respected and valued by teachers, staff, students, families, and the community.					
9.	Families and community members perceive the school as warm, inviting, and helpful.					
10.	Communication (language and tone) is respectful and maintains dignity of the individual (e.g., yelling vs. speaking authoritatively).					

Figure 7.2. *(Continued)*

IV. Learning/Cognitive Environment

An environment that promotes learning and self-fulfillment	Rating				Comments
Indicators:	**1**	**2**	**3**	**4**	
1.	Expectations are high for all students. All are encouraged to succeed.					
2.	The emphasis is on student-centered learning so all types of intelligence and competence are respected and supported.					
3.	Instructional methods respect the different ways children learn.					
4.	Supportive teaching practices are consistently evident (constructive feedback, academic challenges, individual attention, encouragement for positive risk-taking, and opportunities to demonstrate knowledge and skills in a variety of ways).					
5.	The ratio of students in special education is proportionate to the school population, as are allocation of resources to support learning.					
6.	Progress is monitored regularly and shared with families or partners.					
7.	Results of assessments are promptly communicated to students and parents to promote course correction and continuous improvement.					
8.	Results of assessments are used to evaluate and redesign teaching procedures and content.					
9.	Achievements and performance are rewarded, praised, and publicly displayed.					
10.	Teachers or instructors demonstrate skills and knowledge to engage and motivate students and families to participate in the learning.					

#	Indicator			
11.	Families are engaged to have a say and be an integral part of decision making on issues affecting their children's education.			
12.	Support for personal growth of families is offered in terms of their knowledge of child development and parenting skills as well as their own self-esteem.			
13.	Parents and community members are welcomed and recognized as learners. Programs and services are available to meet these needs.			

V. Moral Environment

An environment that promotes values, ethical behavior, and character building	Rating				Comments
Indicators:	1	2	3	4	
1. The school culture (organization's atmosphere and moral code) reflects the values, norms, and expected behaviors for all youth and adults in its responsiveness to the daily tasks and operations.					
2. School and program curricula include development of knowledge/skills that promote ethical decision making, conflict resolution, values clarification, or character education.					
3. There is clear communication around procedures, positive responses, or interventions on topics such as school violence, bullying or teasing, and harassment (sexual or verbal).					
4. There are established policies and rules that support behavior guidance (helping students distinguish right from wrong).					
7. Virtues (e.g., fairness, kindness, cooperation, and sharing) are modeled daily by all staff.					

Figure 7.2. (Continued)

An environment that promotes values, ethical behavior, and character building	Rating				Comments
Indicators:	1	2	3	4	
8. Opportunities exist for youth to:					
question their own moral reasoning and behavior (e.g., peer or mock court, role modeling, active reflection);					
adopt moral habits that will enable them to negotiate the world (e.g., punctuality, meeting deadlines, completing projects);					
get lessons that encourage intrinsic acceptance of prosocial values (e.g., how to treat other people, oneself, and how to regard the process of education);					
discuss the intentions, perspectives, false beliefs, and judgments of characters within a moral dilemma (use contemporary issues); and					
connect to the strength of democracy in society by actively participating in the learning process and construct their own knowledge of social and government systems (e.g., through community service, debates, civic engagement, global citizenship, volunteer work, voter registration).					
9. Parents and schools work together: consensus about values; letters home re: classroom rules and discipline policy; join schoolwide values education efforts; parents participate in moral education programs.					

Source: National Center for Community Schools, *Building Community Schools: A Guide for Action*, 2011

Figure 7.3. Community School Climate Action Planning Tool

I. Physical Environment

An environment that is safe, welcoming, and conducive to learning		Rating					Plan to Improve		
	Indicators:	**1**	**2**	**3**	**4**		**Right Now**	**This Year**	**Next Year**
1.	Space (e.g., library, media center) is shared and accessible to everyone.								
2.	Staff and students are—and feel—safe everywhere on school property.								
3.	Classrooms and grounds are clean and well maintained.								
4.	School equipment is maintained, up-to-date, and available to students, families, or community.								
5.	Class size and ratio of students to teacher are conducive to learning.								
6.	School facilities allow for cocurricular activities.								
7.	Noise level is appropriate for learning and activities being conducted.								
8.	Areas for instruction and activities are appropriate for those uses.								
9.	School and classrooms are visible and inviting (e.g., print-rich displays and work created by students and families).								
10.	School and partner staff members have sufficient books and supplies to maximize participation of all students.								
11.	Clear rules and norms regarding safety and expected behavior are visually displayed throughout the school.								
Action Plan Time Frame		**Support Needed (Information, Resources, Technical Assistance, etc.)**							

Figure 7.3. *(Continued)*

II. Social Environment

An environment that promotes communication, interactions, and relationship building	Rating				Plan to Improve		
Indicators:	1	2	3	4	Right Now	This Year	Next Year
1. Open, honest, and active communication occurs (teachers and students, teachers and parents, school and community, etc.).							
2. Teachers/staff are collegial. They support and work collaboratively around the achievement and success of the students.							
3. Student groupings are diverse.							
4. Parents and teachers/staff are partners in the educational process.							
5. Decisions are made on-site, with the participation of teachers/staff.							
6. School faculty and staff are open to suggestions (from students, families, community). All stakeholders have opportunities to participate in decision making.							
7. Families are encouraged to participate and develop relationships with the faculty and staff as well as with other families.							
8. There are extracurricular opportunities that emphasize group work and improve ties between students.							
9. Parents/families and community members get involved in the planning and organization of school functions.							
10. Networks of support exist (peer mentors, clubs, family resource centers).							
Action Plan Time Frame	**Support Needed (Information, Resources, Technical Assistance, etc.)**						

III. Affective/Emotional Environment

An environment that promotes a sense of belonging and self-esteem

	Indicators:	Rating				Plan to Improve		
		1	2	3	4	Right Now	This Year	Next Year
1.	Interactions between teachers/staff and students are caring, responsive, supportive, and respectful (also administration to staff, peer-to-peer, staff to families, etc.).							
2.	Students trust teachers and staff.							
3.	Morale is high among teachers and staff.							
4.	Staff, students, and families demonstrate school pride.							
5.	The school values diversity and is welcoming to all cultures.							
6.	Teachers/staff, students, and families are respected and valued.							
7.	Teachers/staff and students and families feel that they are contributing to the success of the school.							
8.	The school is respected and valued by teachers, staff, students, families, and the community.							
9.	Families and community members perceive the school as warm, inviting, and helpful.							
10.	Communication (language and tone) is respectful and maintains dignity of the individual (e.g., yelling vs. speaking authoritatively).							
Action Plan Time Frame		**Support Needed (Information, Resources, Technical Assistance, etc.)**						

Figure 7.3. *(Continued)*

IV. Learning/Cognitive Environment

An environment that promotes learning and self-fulfillment	Rating				Plan to Improve		
Indicators:	1	2	3	4	Right Now	This Year	Next Year
1. Expectations are high for all students. All are encouraged to succeed.							
2. The emphasis is on student-centered learning so all types of intelligence and competence are respected and supported.							
3. Instructional methods respect the different ways children learn.							
4. Supportive teaching practices are consistently evident (constructive feedback, academic challenges, individual attention, encouragement for positive risk-taking, and opportunities to demonstrate knowledge and skills in a variety of ways).							
5. The ratio of students in special education is proportionate to the school population, as are allocation of resources to support learning.							
6. Progress is monitored regularly and shared with families or partners.							
7. Results of assessments are promptly communicated to students and parents to promote course correction and continuous improvement.							
8. Results of assessments are used to evaluate and redesign teaching procedures and content.							
9. Achievements and performance are rewarded, praised, and publicly displayed.							
10. Teachers or instructors demonstrate skills and knowledge to engage and motivate students and families to participate in the learning.							

		Support Needed (Information, Resources, Technical Assistance, etc.)
11.	Families are engaged to have a say and be an integral part of decision making on issues affecting their children's education.	
12.	Support for personal growth of families is offered in terms of their knowledge of child development and parenting skills as well as their own self-esteem.	
13.	Parents and community members are welcomed and recognized as learners. Programs and services are available to meet these needs.	
Action Plan Time Frame		

V. Moral Environment

An environment that promotes values, ethical behavior, and character building								
	Rating					**Plan to Improve**		
Indicators:	1	2	3	4		Right Now	This Year	Next Year
1. The school culture (organization's atmosphere and moral code) reflects the values, norms, and expected behaviors for all youth and adults in its responsiveness to the daily tasks and operations.								
2. School and program curricula include development of knowledge/skills that promote ethical decision making, conflict resolution, values clarification, or character education.								
3. There is clear communication around procedures, positive responses or interventions on topics such as school violence, bullying or teasing, and harassment (sexual or verbal).								
4. There are established policies and rules that support behavior guidance (helping students distinguish right from wrong).								

Figure 7.3. *(Continued)*

An environment that promotes values, ethical behavior, and character building	Rating				Plan to Improve		
Indicators:	1	2	3	4	Right Now	This Year	Next Year
5. Virtues (e.g., fairness, kindness, cooperation, and sharing) are modeled daily by all staff.							
6. Opportunities exist for youth to:							
question their own moral reasoning and behavior (e.g., peer or mock court, role modeling, active reflection);							
adopt moral habits that will enable them to negotiate the world (e.g., punctuality, meeting deadlines, completing projects);							
get lessons that encourage intrinsic acceptance of prosocial values (e.g., how to treat other people, oneself, and how to regard the process of education);							
discuss the intentions, perspectives, false beliefs, and judgments of characters within a moral dilemma (use contemporary issues); and							
connect to the strength of democracy in society by actively participating in the learning process and construct their own knowledge of social and government systems (e.g., through community service, debates, civic engagement, global citizenship, volunteer work, voter registration).							
7. Parents and schools work together: consensus about values; letters home re: classroom rules and discipline policy; join schoolwide values education efforts; parents participate in moral education programs.							

Source: National Center for Community Schools, *Building Community Schools: A Guide for Action,* 2011

CONCLUSION: A CALL FOR VISION AND LEADERSHIP

As authors, we have given much thought to providing essential information on how to launch and sustain a community school initiative. Our circle of friends and colleagues, who have offered their advice and support for this endeavor, have reminded us that we would be remiss to not bring to the attention of readers the importance of vision and leadership in this approach to school reform. A final story, which reflects the importance of both, is shared from Edison's staff retreat held in June 2011.

THE PRINCIPAL'S PERSPECTIVE: RECOLLECTIONS OF SHARED LEADERSHIP IN ACTION

The final staff retreat before my retirement in June 2011 was quite memorable and very moving. As part of a "unity builder" activity, staff members and the assistant superintendent, who had worked so closely with us over the years, were asked to recall a "community school memory" from Edison's fifteen-year history of implementation. Of the many wonderful and sometimes humorous memories that were shared, one particular recollection seems to capture the power of dedicated community school practitioners with a common vision.

Our assistant superintendent remembered how the collective energies of Edison's staff and partners had been impressively mobilized to address the needs of a particular student who had emigrated from Mexico. This child came to Edison with major health concerns but no health coverage. In addition, although he communicated in English reasonably well, he had not attended school for over a year when sent unexpectedly to live with a set of loving grandparents, neither of whom had obtained legal guardianship of the boy. Finally, since parental contact could not be established, the school's staff had no access to the child's prior educational records.

The assistant superintendent recalled sitting in on a meeting with school staff, grandparents, and partners as they pooled their knowledge and resources. Over the course of a year, this "whole child" plan of action served to demonstrate the potential of cross-boundary leadership and collaboration in community schools.

The family caseworker was able to take the lead role in helping the grandparents to pursue the appropriate legal channels for them to secure custody of the child. Staff from the school-based health center then attended to the child's medical needs, while school staff provided academic intervention services at the classroom level.

At my final retreat, a year later, the child's current teacher joyously wept as she reported on his progress in terms of his overall well-being, social-emotional maturation, positive attitude toward school, and learning. Over the

course of my tenure as principal of the Thomas Edison Elementary School,
this scenario would be repeated many times over.

This personal perspective clearly conveys an important message of the
book about the critical role of leadership and strong dedication to a philosophy of Whole Child Education in the community school. However, it is also
essential to underscore the role of the principal in standing at the forefront
of change, with a strengths-based orientation to working with staff, parents,
partners, and children. The position of principal in the community school
requires balancing several roles, managing multiple tasks, and working collaboratively with a wide variety of stakeholders.

In closing, we recommend that schools and districts planning to implement
the community school strategy take advantage of the many resources in the
field with a focus on professional development and leadership development.
We also ask readers to return to the title and sub-title of our book as we encourage them to take a whole child approach to transforming their schools
into community schools with district support and commitment for "turning
every school into a community school". While the work appears daunting,
the theoretical case for working in this comprehensive and integrated way is
very strong as is the growing body of empirical evidence of the effectiveness
of this approach. Armed with this knowledge, practitioners can feel confident
that "*community schools are the right way to go*" and inspired in their work to
prepare all of our nation's young people for productive adulthood.

RELATED RESOURCES: COMMUNITY SCHOOLS, FAMILY ENGAGEMENT, CHARACTER EDUCATION, AND PROFESSIONAL DEVELOPMENT SCHOOLS

Listed below are selected readings, organizations, and other resources that
provide valuable information, research, and/or technical assistance related to
community schools, family engagement, professional development schools,
and character education.

ORGANIZATIONS OFFERING TECHNICAL SUPPORT AND ADVOCACY FOR COMMUNITY SCHOOLS

Coalition for Community Schools

http://www.communityschools.org

An alliance of national, state, and local organizations whose mission is to mobilize the resources and capacity of multiple sectors and institutions to create a united movement for community schools.

Important Publications:

- "Scaling Up School and Community Partnerships: The Community Schools Strategy" (2011). Downloadable at: http://www.communityschools.org/scalingup
- "Financing Community Schools" (2010). Downloadable at: http://www.communityschools.org/assets/1/AssetManager/finance-paper.pdf
- "Growing Community Schools: The Role of Cross-Boundary Leadership" (2006). Downloadable at: http://www.community schools.org/assets/1/AssetManager/CBLFinal.pdf http://www.communityschools.org/assets/1/AssetManager/finance-paper.pdf
- "Making the Difference: Research & Practice in Community Schools" (2003). Downloadable at: http://www.community schools.org/assets/1/Page/CCSFullReport.pdf

National Center for Community Schools

www.nationalcenterforcommunityschools.org

Part of the Children's Aid Society, the Center is a practice-based organization providing technical support and assistance for the implementation of community schools around the United States and abroad.

Important Publications (all available at www.nationalcenterfor communityschool.org):

- "Building Community Schools: A Guide for Action (2011). A detailed manual that outlines the essential steps in developing an effective community school.

- Partnership Press. A quarterly newsletter that explores critical themes in community school implementation.
- Community School Fact Sheet series:
  - "Community Schools: Frequently Asked Questions"
  - "Community Schools: Research Base"
  - "Community Schools: Results to Date"
  - "Sustainability Case Study"
- "The Four Critical Capacities of Community Schools." Four critical capacities shared by successful community schools of all models, around which the Center's technical assistance is organized.

Selected Readings on Community Schools

- *Full-Service Schools* by Joy Dryfoos. Jossey-Bass, 1994.
  A classic in the field, by community schools' champion Joy Dryfoos.
- *Community Schools in Action: Lessons from a Decade of Practice* coedited by Joy Dryfoos, Jane Quinn, and Carol Barkin. Oxford University Press, 2005.
  A synthesis of lessons from the first ten years of operations at Children's Aid Community Schools.
- *Community Schools: A Strategy for Integrating Youth Development and School Reform* by Joy Dryfoos and Jane Quinn, eds. New Directions for Youth Development, Fall 2005. This volume summarizes the experiences of the Children's Aid Society community schools and additional community school models, including Beacons, University-Assisted, Chicago school-system community schools, and more.
- *Organizing Schools for Improvement: Lessons from Chicago* by Anthony S. Bryk, Penny Bender Sebring, Elaine Allensworth, Stuart Luppescu, and John Q. Easton. University of Chicago Press, 2010.
  Anthony Bryk and colleagues at the Consortium on Chicago School Research determined that five "essential elements" are necessary for schools to improve. These include:
  1. Strong principal leadership in driving change
  2. Authentic family and community engagement
  3. The school's ability to build professional capacity
  4. Student-centered school climate
  5. Coherent curriculum

- *Kids First: Five Big Ideas for Transforming Children's Lives and America's Future* by David Kirp. Public Affairs, 2011. Researcher David Kirp devotes one chapter to community schools as an important strategy for policymakers to address to in improving outcomes for youth.

Resources and Selected Readings on Parent and Family Engagement

- Harvard Family Research Project
  http://hfrp.org
  This Harvard-based research team focuses on three components of complementary learning: early care and education, out-of-school time, and family and community involvement in education.
  Important Publications:
  Beyond Random Acts: Family, School, and Community Engagement as an Integral Part of Education Reform by Heather Weiss, M. Elena Lopez, and Heidi Rosenberg. Harvard Family Research Project, 2010.
  Downloadable at: http://hfrp.org/BeyondRandomActs
  Beyond Random Acts:
  1. Provides a research-based framework for family engagement;
  2. Examines the policy levers that can drive change in promoting systemic family, school, and community engagement;
  3. Focuses on data systems as a powerful tool to engage families for twenty-first-century student learning; and
  4. Examines the integral role of families in transforming low-performing schools.
- *School, Family, and Community Partnerships: Your Handbook for Action, Third Edition* by Joyce Epstein and Associates. Corwin Press, 2009.
  This practical handbook provides a detailed framework for how schools, districts, and state leaders can develop more effective programs for family and community involvement.
- *Beyond the Bake Sale: The Essential Guide to Family-School Partnerships* by Anne T. Henderson, Karen L. Mapp, Vivian R. Johnson, and Don Davies. The New Press, 2007.
  Written for parents, teachers, administrators, and policymakers, this practical guide provides useful tools, checklists, sample surveys, and school policies for promoting community and family involvement in the educational process.

Resources for Character Education

Textbox 7.4.

Character Education Partnership (CEP)

www.character.org

This organization provides valuable information on implementing quality character education by holding annual conferences, advocating for this effort in legislation, recognizing exemplary programs, and producing a number of related publications and videos.

Developmental Studies Center

www.devstu.org

This nonprofit organization was the developer of the original "Child Development Program" and has since expanded to provide a wide array of research-based programs that focus on the development of academic skills, prosocial behaviors, and creating a caring school community.

Responsive Classroom

www.responsiveclassroom.org

This comprehensive approach to character education, which integrates community building and academic skills, provides professional development and publishes numerous guides for implementation.

Organizations Supporting Professional Development Schools

- National Association of Professional Development Schools (NAPDS)
    www.NAPDS.org
    This organization holds annual conferences with hands-on, practical presentations and opportunities for networking. Conference content is appropriate for university and preK through twelfth educators with an exclusive focus on issues relevant to Professional Development Schools.
    Important Publication:
    School-University Partnerships (journal publication)

The journal of the National Association for Professional Development Schools is nationally disseminated and contains articles written by both university and school educators that highlight policies and practices in school-university partnerships.
- Manhattanville College, School of Education
  www.mville.edu
  Professional Development Schools Consortium
  A network of Professional Development Schools devoted to improving teaching preparation, the professional development of practicing teachers, and research and inquiry in schools with a diverse student population.

Selected Readings on Professional Development Schools

Textbox 7.5.

Professional Development Schools: Schools for Developing a Profession by Linda Darling-Hammond. Teachers College Press, 1994.
Explains the function, structure, and philosophy of the professional development school. The text includes case studies, taken from urban and suburban settings, that illustrate the accomplishments of these schools as well as the challenges they face as they strive to create a new and viable vision for the improvement of the American educational system.

Professional Development Schools Research: Advances in Community Thought and Research, Volume 3 by I. Guadarrama, J. Ramsey, and J. Nath (eds.). Charlotte, NC: Information Age Publishing, 2008.
Research in Professional Development Schools Series includes collection of organized papers that represent the best and latest examples of practitioner thinking, research, and program design and evaluation in the field at the national level.

The Professional Development Schools Handbook: Starting, Sustaining, and Assessing Partnerships That Improve Student Learning by Lee Teitel. Thousand Oaks, CA: Corwin Press, 2003.
This manual is a resource to help fulfill these goals and more. Structured around the five Standards for Professional Development Schools developed by the National Council for the Accreditation of Teacher Education (NCATE).

Standards for Professional Development Schools by NCATE. 2001.
This publication contains the five core standards for PDS, along with developmental guidelines to assist PDS partners as they move from one stage of development to the next. The standards were developed to strengthen PDS implementation. They are designed for use in an assessment process and to provide feedback to PDS partners about their work.

Professional Development Schools: Enhancing Teacher Quality by Richard Ishler (ed.). Research for Better Schools, 2008.
The book is organized around the NCATE standards for PDS. It is the result of four years of work initiated by the Pennsylvania Academy for the Profession of Teaching and Learning.

References

Association for Supervision and Curriculum Development. (2007). *The learning compact redefined: A call to action. A report of the commission on the whole child.* Alexandria, VA.

Berkowitz, M. W., and Bier, M. C. (2005). *What works in character education: A report for policy makers and opinion leaders.* Washington, DC: Character Education Partnership.

Berliner, D. (2007). Our impoverished view of educational reform. In *Sociology of education: A critical reader*, ed. Alan Sadovnik. New York: Routledge.

Blank, M. J., Berg, A. C., and Melaville, A. (2006, April). *Growing community schools: The role of cross-boundary leadership.* Washington, DC: Coalition for Community Schools.

Blank, M. J., Jacobson, R., Melaville, A., and Pearson, S. (2010, November). *Financing community schools: Leveraging resources to support student success.* Washington, DC: Coalition for Community Schools.

Blank, M. J., Melaville, A., and Shah, B. (2003). *Making the difference: Research and practice in community schools.* Coalition for Community Schools. Retrieved March 29, 2005, from www.communityschools.org/assets/1/Page/CCSFullReport.pdf.

Boston College Center for Child, Family and Community Partnerships. (2010). *City connects: The lasting impact of optimized student support.* Boston, MA.

Brickman, E., Cancelli, A., and Sanchez, A. (1998). *The Children's Aid Society/Board of Education community schools: Second-year evaluation report.* New York, NY: Fordham University.

Bronfenbrenner, U. (1979). *The ecology of human development: Experiments by nature and design.* Cambridge, MA: Harvard University Press.

Bryk, A. S., and Schneider, B. (2002). *Trust in schools: A core resource for improvement.* New York: Russell Sage Foundation.

Bryk, A. S., Sebring, P. B., Allensworth, E., Luppescu, S., and Easton, J. Q. (2010). Organizing schools for improvement: Lessons from Chicago. Chicago, IL: University of Chicago Press.

Carnegie Council on Adolescent Development. (1992). *A matter of time: Risk and opportunity in the nonschool hours.* New York.

Character Education Partnership. (2010). *Eleven principles of character education.* Washington, D.C.

Children's Aid Society. (2001). *Building a community school.* New York: The Children's Aid Society.

Clark, H. et al. (2008). *Young adolescents learn and thrive in after-school programs: Results of a three-year evaluation in six New York City middle schools.* New York: ActKnowledge, Center for Human Environments, City University of New York.

Clark, H. et al. (2009). *Study comparing Children's Aid Society community schools to other New York City public schools (all schools and peer schools).* New York: ActKnowledge, Center for Human Environments, City University of New York.

Clark, H., and Engle, R. (2000). *Summary of research findings.* New York: ActKnowledge, Center for Human Environments, City University of New York.

Clark, H., and Engle, R. (2003). *The Children's Aid Society's community school mental health services analysis of progress in 4th year of the New York state education department's VESID—effective practices contract.* New York: ActKnowledge, Center for Human Environments, City University of New York.

Clark, R. M. (1988). *Critical factors in why disadvantaged students succeed or fail in school.* New York: Academy for Educational Development.

Coalition for Community Schools. (2009). *Community schools research report 2009.* Washington, DC.

Coalition for Community Schools. (2011). *Policy brief on the reauthorization of the Elementary and Secondary Education Act.* Washington, DC.

Cummins. J. (1981). Age on arrival and immigrant second language acquisition in Canada: A reassessment. *Applied Linguistics 2*: 132–49.

Darling-Hammond, L. (1994). *Professional development schools: Schools for developing a profession.* New York: Teachers College Press.

Developmental Studies Center. (1995a). *At home in our schools.* Oakland, CA.

Developmental Studies Center. (1995b). *Homeside activities.* Oakland, CA.

Developmental Studies Center. (1997). *Blueprints for a collaborative classroom.* Oakland, CA.

Developmental Studies Center. (2004). *Caring school community.* Oakland, CA.

Dryfoos, J. G. (1998). *Safe passage: Making it through adolescence in a risky society.* New York: Oxford University Press.

Dryfoos, J. G., Quinn, J., and Barkin, C. (2005). *Community schools in action: Lessons from a decade of practice.* New York: Oxford University Press.

Duncan, A. (2009). *Every school a community school: A vision implant.* Keynote Address by the U.S. Secretary of Education at The Children's Aid Society National Center for Community Schools Community Schools Practicum, October 22.

Eccles, J. S. (1999). The development of children ages 6 to 14. *The Future of Children 9*(2): 30–44.

Ferrara, J., and Santiago, E. (2007). Crossroads: Where community meets character in the pursuit of academic excellence. *The Journal of Research in Character Education 5*(1): 95–101.

Finance Project. (2007). *Thinking broadly: Financing strategies for youth programs.* Washington, DC.

Fullan, M. (2007). *The new meaning of educational change.* New York: Teachers College Press.

ICF International. (2010). *Communities in schools national evaluation: Five-year executive summary.* Fairfax, VA.

Ladd, H. F., and Fiske, E. B. (2011). Class matters: Why won't we admit it?, *New York Times,* December 12, A23.

Langford, B. H., and Flynn-Khan, M. (2003). *Sustainability planning workbook.* Washington, DC: The Finance Project.

London, M. (1995). *Achieving performance excellence in university administrations: A team approach to organizational change and employee development.* Santa Barbara, CA: Praeger.

Martin, M., Fergus, E., and Noguera, P. (2010). Responding to the needs of the whole child: A case study of a high-performing elementary school for immigrant children. *Reading & Writing Quarterly 26*(3): 195–222.

Maslow, A. (1962). *Toward a psychology of being.* Princeton, NJ: Van Nostrand.

Mayer, B. (2004). *Beyond neutrality: Confronting the crisis in conflict resolution.* San Francisco, CA: Jossey-Bass.

Mitchell, M. (2011). *Cincinnati community learning centers: Performance evaluation 2011.* Cincinnati: CPS Community Learning Centers.

National Center for Community Schools. (2011). *Building community schools: A guide for action.* New York.

National Center on Response to Intervention. (2010). *Essential components of RTI— A closer look at response to intervention.* Retrieved October 7, 2010, from http://www.rti4success.org.

Nelson, J., Lott, L., and Glenn, H. S. (2000). *Positive discipline in the classroom.* California: Prima Publishing.

Noddings, N. (2008). All our students thinking. *Educational Leadership 65*(5): 8–13.

Noguera, P. (2003). *City schools and the American dream: Reclaiming the promise of public education.* New York: Teachers College Press.

OMG Center for Collaborative Learning. (2010). *Hartford community schools evaluation: Findings from year 2.* Philadelphia, PA.

Rahim, M. A. (2001). *Managing conflict in organizations.* Westport, CT: Quorum Books.

Ravitch, D. (2010). *The death and life of the great American school system: How testing and choice are undermining education.* New York: Basic Press.

Rees, F. (2001). *How to lead work teams: Facilitation skills.* San Francisco, CA: Jossey-Bass.

Reschely, D. J., and Hosp, J. L. (2004). State SLD identification policies and practices. *Learning Disabilities Quarterly 27*: 197–213.

Rogers, J. S. (1998). *Community schools: Lessons from the past and present.* Flint, MI: Charles S. Mott Foundation.

Schaps, E., Battistich, V., and Solomon, D. (2004). Community in school as key to student growth: Findings from the child development project. In *Building academic success on social and emotional learning: What does the research say?* eds. Zins, J., Weissberg, R., Wang, M., and Walberg, H. New York: Teacher's College Press.

Shonkoff, J. P., and Phillips, D. A. (2000). *From neurons to neighborhoods: The science of early childhood.* Washington, DC: National Academy Press.

Snow, R. N., and Phillips, P. H. (2007). *Making critical decisions: A practical guide for non-profit organizations.* San Francisco, CA: Jossey-Bass.

Stone, C. (2001). *Building civic capacity.* Lawrence: University of Kansas Press.

U.S. Department of Education Office of Safe and Drug-Free Schools. (n.d.). *Charter education . . . Our shared responsibility.* Retrieved October 7, 2010, from http://www2.ed.gov/admins/lead/character/brochure.pdf.

Vygotsky, L. S. (1978). *Mind in society: The development of higher psychological processes.* Cambridge, MA: Harvard University Press.

Wepner, S. B., and Hopkins, D. (2011). *Collaborative leadership in action: Partnering for success in schools.* New York: Teachers College Press.

Zeichner, K. (1996). Designing educative practicum experiences for prospective teachers. In *Currents of reform in preservice teacher education,* eds. Zeichner, K., Melnick, S., and Gomez, M. L., 215–34. New York: Teachers College Press.

Zins, J., Weissberg, R., Wang, M., and Walberg, H., eds. *Building academic success on social and emotional learning: What does the research say?* New York: Teachers College Press.

A mural created by the children in the SER/Edison after school program around Edison's vision of a community school. This mural was displayed at a community health fair at the school and still hangs in the reception area of the Open Door Family Medical Center, one of Edison's long-standing community partners.